Redemptive Scale

What Scale Is, And How God Can Use It.

GARY WILKINS

WESTBOW
PRESS®
A DIVISION OF THOMAS NELSON
& ZONDERVAN

WestBow Press books may be ordered through booksellers or by contacting:

WestBow Press
A Division of Thomas Nelson & Zondervan
1663 Liberty Drive
Bloomington, IN 47403
www.westbowpress.com
844-714-3454

ISBN: 979-8-3850-3008-8 (sc)
ISBN: 979-8-3850-3009-5 (e)

Library of Congress Control Number: 2024915136

Print information available on the last page.

WestBow Press rev. date: 09/16/2024

Dedication

I am so honored and excited to share this story and the ideas it illustrates with you. I am deeply grateful to those who have made this book possible.

- Mark Snyder's wife, Carol, allowed me to share his story and provided gracious encouragement throughout the writing and publishing process.
- David Snyder, Mark's son and the executive director of Sustainable Medical Missions, dreamed with me about what the story could mean and provided all the information and connections that made telling it possible.
- Selin Waltz and Doug Walouke, Sustainable Medical Missions board members, generously shared their own experiences with Mark and their excitement about being part of the organization he created.
- Emmanuel Ndolimana, Lincoln Chirochierwa, and Stephen Mwatha opened up their lives to let me get to know Mark and Sustainable Med through their experiences.

Faithful friends also helped me in the writing process, giving me room to think and challenging me to be better.

- Seth Morgan, my employer at MLA Companies, introduced me to the concept of scale through a biblical framework and has supported my work.
- Zeke Swift, Steve Schwandner, and Kent Schellhause discussed my ideas with me and carefully read my first draft, providing invaluable encouragement and direction.

- My mom, Merle Wilkins, read every draft and allowed me to talk endlessly about the story. Her engagement and support kept me going.
- My wife, Leigh, is my most faithful friend and supporter. She protected the time I needed to complete this project and encouraged me to see it through. When I had done all I could, Leigh applied her exceptional skills as a medical writer and editor to polish the text.

And, for bringing each of these people into my life...

> *"...thanks be to God, who gives us the victory through our Lord Jesus Christ."*
>
> *-1 Corinthians 15:57*

Contents

Introduction

Scale is the phenomenon of an organization growing big and has become a fact of modern life. The words on this page, in whatever form you are reading them, are a product of scale. So are countless things we use every day, from clean water and electricity to the weather and traffic apps on your phone.

For Christians, faith is a fact of life. I would argue that even if you don't believe in God, you believe in something. As human beings, we cannot function without a way to explain and connect to things beyond ourselves.

Christianity is an ancient faith. We look back to the first moments of creation to find our link to the God who created us. And we strive every day to apply that ancient faith to our modern, scaling world.

Faith and scale are in tension and often seem to work against each other. Because of that tension, we are constantly being pushed to separate our lives between our sacred faith and the secular world of scale.

But what if we could harness that tension to scale something truly worthwhile? Can we create something that resonates with the proclamation of the first Creator that is "very good"?

The solution is to understand scale through a biblical framework. Then, we can assess how it works and identify the key opportunities to turn scale toward good as God defines it. Scale is not the enemy, nor is it the solution to every problem. But scale is an entry point into the bigger question of how God works in the world.

This book examines the modern phenomenon of scale through the ancient truths of the Bible. In the process, I will develop a biblical framework for scale, describe a cycle that explains how scale works, and identify guiding principles for using scale for good.

But first, a true story of scale that starts in a Cincinnati hospital and ends with a medical movement in Africa.

What if...

- Government partnered with Christian leaders to help people change self-destructive behaviors.
- People who cared for others could overcome a culture of indifference and suspicion.
- Christians could help eliminate institutional waste and corruption.
- We could find community that welcomed us as we are and made us better people.
- Leaders from other faiths asked Christians to teach their people because of the love they brought.
- There was a compelling way to bring the gospel to millions of people who lived within sight of a church but had never experienced the love of Jesus.

It sounds like a fantasy, or at least a wish list for a world other than the one we live in today.

But these things are happening, and I don't just mean in isolated pockets or one-off anecdotes. An entire nation is being transformed, and others are following its lead.

This is transformation at scale!

A True Story

When I say scale, you may expect to find a big-name organization or well-known leader. That's what scale looks like in our everyday experience.

But I'm talking about a different organization that you've probably never heard of. And if you look for the visionary who started it, you'll only encounter his spirit, which lives on in many unexpected ways.

That visionary is a doctor from Cincinnati, Ohio, who followed Jesus. The organization is not in America but in a small country in Africa. And at its heart is physical healing from simple diseases.

This healing doesn't happen through a miracle but by simple actions such as bringing clean water and good hygiene to some of the poorest places in the world. Yet great faith has been required to perform these simple acts, and only the love of God can account for their impact.

Yet this is not another program to dig wells or bring medicine to remote villages. Rather, it is an organization in which local people empowered by God's love solve their own problems.

This organization is Sustainable Medical Missions, founded by Dr. Mark Snyder, and its unique approach to scale created a movement that has changed millions of lives.

Scale vs. Movement

One of scale's most powerful effects is the creation of movements. In a movement, people do more with a product or service than even the original developers had in mind. Particularly successful products and services start cultural trends that both drive demand and raise expectations.

Movements:

- Grow exponentially and draw energy from sources outside the group or organization that started it.
- Form when people take ownership of an idea and use it for a greater purpose.
- Are powerful and cannot be controlled.

Scale:

- Can be controlled.
- Works when key steps happen.
- Has the power to transform lives for the better.
- Can be a catalyst for movements.

My focus is not merely on making scale work but on how it can be a force for good by creating movements. As we delve deeper, we'll discover how scale triggers cultural, individual, and community changes, all of which are integral to the formation of movements.

With the right understanding of scale, we can consider how God might use scale to start movements for his glory.

What Good is Scale?

We live in a world of scale. Scale is the phenomenon of an organization growing exponentially. In its simplest form, growth is addition, but scale is multiplication.

Many businesses and organizations are no longer content with the standard growth-by-addition of days gone by. They now want the multiplication promised by scale.

We've become used to products that grow quickly from nothing to massive success or individuals who go from invisibility to notoriety overnight. We seem to have proven we can scale almost anything. But should we?

Our experience with scale is mixed. We can make the mistake of forgetting the improvements brought by scale in the past and only focus on the latest set of problems it creates.

We understand scale in economic terms because of the financial value it creates, but Scripture does not measure our work that way. God most values people, who are created in his image.

So how do we scale something truly good that cares for people and doesn't just make life easier? Why can't these methods accomplish something that will transform people's lives for eternity?

To apply scale to accomplishing good, we must understand what makes it happen. In particular, we must identify the type of scale that becomes a movement for what the Bible defines as good. I call that Redemptive Scale.

The story in this book illustrates how God can scale the impact of someone who values people as he does.

About This Book

This book is written in three parts.

1. **How Sustainable Medical Missions Scaled.** This dramatic story demonstrates how God uses scale to solve one of the world's biggest problems. This small organization has scaled something considered impossible by some of the best minds and best-funded organizations.

2. **What Is Scale?** You'll learn why scale has become the focus of business and how that fits with God's plan for the world. And you'll develop an understanding of scale through a Biblical framework and see how this scale works in the world and in Sustainable Med.

3. **How God Uses Scale.** We will apply scale to this question: How do we love and care for others? We will examine each guiding principle for Redemptive Scale and work through the practical implications, and look at how Sustainable Med used Redemptive Scale to create a movement to love and care for others.

Scale has implications for business and ministry, and I've served in both. In my experience, pastors need businesspeople to remove some of the mystery from scale, and businesspeople need pastors to restore some of its majesty.

My prayer is that you will be inspired to trust God for bigger things and that through you he will do more than you can ask or imagine (Eph. 3:20).

PART 1
How Sustainable Med Scaled

2

Zero in on Zero

A Frustrated Vision

Dr. Mark Snyder couldn't understand why his colleagues wouldn't believe him.

As an orthopedic surgeon in Cincinnati, Ohio, he was implementing a revolutionary change in patient care to prevent post-surgical infections. The evidence was there; his colleagues admitted that. And he had done everything he could to win them to his side. But they still insisted on doing things the same way as before.

Maybe he was the problem. Perhaps they were turned off by his enthusiasm and excitement. Or maybe it was more profound than that. Mark wondered if the issue was his Christian faith. Did they think he was trying to get them to agree with his beliefs?

"He was frustrated and excited," Mark's son David remembers. "He really believed he had a solution that would change people's lives, but the others weren't getting it."

In Mark's case, this could literally be a matter of life and death. Post-surgical infections lead to illness and sometimes death, as well as millions of dollars in healthcare costs.

Mark felt an intense burden to implement his plan. He couldn't ignore the sense that God was calling him to do it and had prepared him for this task. That conviction was the source of his determination.

What happened in the months and years ahead would prove that Mark was right. But the path and destination weren't what he had envisioned.

Excellent Care

Mark didn't enter medicine to solve problems related to post-surgical infections. Nor did he anticipate that trying to minimize complications related to orthopedic surgery would alter the trajectory of his life. But he did want to provide the best care for his patients.

Mark graduated from the University of Cincinnati College of Medicine in 1979 and specialized in orthopedic surgery, sports medicine, and adult reconstructive orthopedic surgery. He built a successful practice in Cincinnati while serving as an elder in his church and with various nonprofits.

Then, in 2008, a teaching hospital in Cincinnati hired Mark to optimize every aspect of patient care in its joint replacement surgery program. The clinic also hired Kathy Eten, a respected nurse, to develop and implement the program under Mark's direction.

Mark prayed for his patients regularly, and he began praying that God would show him how to bring about changes in the clinic so every patient received excellent care.

One night, God woke Mark up with a simple idea. What if they looked beyond the specific problems he was trying to solve? What if they asked what happened before, during, and after joint replacement surgery? That would give greater insight into how those problems could be avoided altogether.

Pursuing Zero

The problems Mark was trying to avoid were a variety of complications associated with hip and knee replacements. This included everything from patient falls to post-surgical infections.[1]

---

[1] Resources and outside documents can be found at RedemptiveScale.com/Resources.

Using evidence-based research, Mark and Kathy identified the top 10 hip and knee replacement complications, called adverse events, and set a target of zero incidents. They reviewed the medical literature to identify best practices to eliminate the factors before, during, and after each targeted adverse event.

The "Zero in on Zero" program was born.

It included everything from pre-surgery nutrition to post-surgical follow-up and the many small decisions the care team made in between. Mark and Kathy also asked the other surgeons and nurses to weigh in.

Then, they evaluated each surgeon's procedures and decided which were the best at reducing the adverse events to zero. "Zero in on Zero" asked what happens before, during, and after these adverse events. The care team replaced practices that contributed to these adverse events with practices that helped avoid them. The goal was zero adverse events in the clinic.

Mark had to convince all the other people who could reduce these factors to buy into his preventative approach. This included everyone from hospital administrators to the housekeeping staff.

Unbeknownst to him, Mark had taken his first steps toward developing something much bigger than a well-run joint replacement program.

Changing the Culture in the Clinic

The hospital was behind "Zero in on Zero," or ZIOZ (*Zy*-oz). But some individual surgeons were resistant. Even after seeing the evidence supporting the new procedures, they did things the way they were used to.

Why? One reason was that the U.S. medical system holds surgeons responsible for their patient's care. As a result, the surgeons expected to have complete control over how they conducted their procedures. This created a culture in which surgeons were not questioned about their decisions.

However, the point of ZIOZ was to collectively find the best procedures by getting input from everyone who interacted with a patient before, during, and after surgery. Unfortunately, this approach ran directly against the prevailing culture in the orthopedic clinic.

Mark was a respected orthopedic surgeon. But he was also a deeply committed Christ-follower. Kathy was also a believer, and her faith had been a key reason Mark chose her to work with him on ZIOZ.

As a Christian, Mark had learned humility, which meant he was predisposed to acknowledge his dependence on God and seek input from others. Those who did not have the same faith as Mark struggled to reconcile his humility with what they expected from him as an accomplished surgeon.

Building A Community of Caregivers

As ZIOZ gained momentum, the surgeons in the orthopedic clinic were required to participate as part of their contracts. However, some were still resistant and openly criticized the effort.

But another group did buy in. Mark's goals and approach in ZIOZ deeply resonated with the surgical nurses in the clinic.

The nurses saw how each surgeon's approach before ZIOZ affected patients during and after surgery. The impact wasn't always positive, but nurses had no authority to question the surgeons. They had to follow the surgeon's chosen procedures, regardless of what the nurse thought was best.

This variance in procedures required the nurses to assume a slightly different professional identity with each surgeon. Doing so made nurses valuable to the individual surgeons, but limited their ability to work together.

This work environment strained relationships among the nurses because even though they noticed the differences in patient outcomes, they could do little to improve them. With ZIOZ, Kathy had the authority to take the nurses' observations into consideration. She and Mark used their insights to develop best practices in the clinic.

This created a sense of community for the nurses because they now had reason to talk about what they observed and had a central role in achieving the goal of zero adverse events. ZIOZ also empowered nurses to give input to surgeons because they could speak with a unified voice and support each other as they worked toward shared ZIOZ objectives.

This sense of community among the nurses created a powerful incentive for the surgeons to adhere to the ZIOZ procedures.

ZIOZ Gains Influence

Under Mark's leadership, ZIOZ demonstrated remarkable results, including something unexpected. As the various surgeons began to use ZIOZ processes, they noticed that the effects multiplied each other. Combining two or more procedures created more significant synergies than each individual procedure did on its own.

Although some surgeons were only hesitantly participating, the nursing team had formed a community to support the program. Eventually, everyone on the orthopedic team moved toward zero incidents of the 10 types of adverse events Mark and Kathy had identified.

However, factors outside the orthopedic nursing unit prevented them from reaching zero adverse events. For example, some instructions during the patient's hospital intake conflicted with the procedures that ZIOZ had identified. As a result, Mark and Kathy approached other departments in the hospital to identify where staff members could contribute to ZIOZ.

But getting other departments on board took hard work. Some were very supportive, but others were not. One department that chose to participate was housekeeping. Asking for input from the janitors in a medical program was revolutionary.

Their observations were particularly relevant to patient falls. The housekeeping staff saw the patients when the doctors and nurses weren't around. As a result, they could prevent a patient from getting out of bed and call a nurse before the patient fell, avoiding an adverse event.

As these other departments began cooperating, ZIOZ moved closer to its goal of zero complications. This progress created opportunities for Mark and Kathy to speak at conferences and share their experience.

Soon, other orthopedic programs began to study ZIOZ and deploy it. With Kathy's help, Mark began publishing medical articles that demonstrated the impact of ZIOZ.

Reaching Zero

Zero In On Zero was working! The ZIOZ team was seeing the incidence of the 10 adverse events drop lower and lower. Then, after several years of work, it happened. "We reached 0% in all 10 areas," Kathy recalls. "That was an amazing day because no one thought we could do it!"

ZIOZ was never a short-term effort to attain a one-time goal. It was a new, sustainable way of doing orthopedic surgery that would influence other programs and hospitals worldwide.

ZIOZ helped the orthopedic surgery program receive its first Gold Seal of Approval certification from The Joint Commission in 2011. The clinic was one of the first to achieve this and helped many other hospitals do the same.

ZIOZ would eventually influence orthopedic surgery worldwide and other medical procedures beyond orthopedics. The approach pioneered by ZIOZ became part of what is now known as integrated clinical pathways. It is built into modern hospitals' digital information systems.

Scale or Movement?

Despite ZIOZ achieving its goal of zero adverse events, Mark was not satisfied. He wanted to change lives, not just procedures. ZIOZ certainly scaled, but it failed to create the movement in patient care Mark had hoped it would.

ZIOZ could not change doctors' attitudes toward their patients and the other people involved in patient care. Mark's approach had been to empower people at all levels of healthcare to act on their personal concerns for patients. But ZIOZ was instead absorbed into the computer programming that dictated these care providers' decisions.

This massively helped ZIOZ's scale, but it was exactly the opposite of the movement in healthcare Mark had hoped to spark. Mark's identity as a Christ-follower meant that he wanted to impact others for eternity, not just for their health in this life.

Mark relied on God's leading to accomplish what he did through ZIOZ, but that's not all God had placed on Mark's heart to do.

The Challenge of NTDs

How To Cure One Billion People?

The next phase in Mark's journey began in 2010 when he saw an article titled "How To Cure 1 Billion People?" by Dr. Peter Hotez in *Scientific American*. As a doctor, Mark was intrigued. Then, as he read further, he became excited.

The article was about neglected tropical diseases affecting one billion people worldwide. These diseases are simple infections; in most cases, they can be cured relatively easily. However, many factors make it impossible to bring these cures to people at scale.

One of ZIOZ's most significant achievements had been eradicating post-surgical infection with existing resources. Mark fostered cooperation to make it work.

Could that same approach be applied, and could ZIOZ be scaled to help cure a billion people of neglected tropical diseases?

What are NTDs?

According to the World Health Organization, "neglected tropical diseases (NTDs) are a diverse group of 20 conditions that are mainly prevalent in tropical areas, where they mostly affect impoverished communities and disproportionately affect women and children. These diseases cause devastating health, social, and economic consequences to more than one billion people."

Current estimates place the world's population at just under 8 billion people. That means every eighth person is afflicted with an NTD. The effects of these diseases have impacted entire countries. NTDs have created some of the most economically devastated areas of the world.

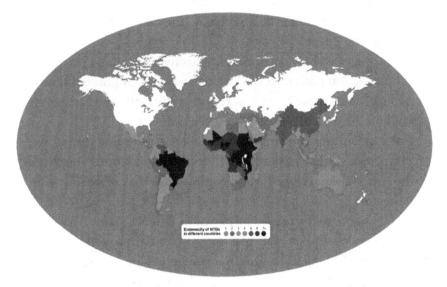

The Impact of Neglected Tropical Diseases Globally.[2]

To put that in perspective, the entire population of the Americas, including North, Central, and South America is estimated at just over one billion people. Imagine every one of those people suffering from "devastating health, social and economic consequences."

The Disease of Neglect

The vast majority of people with NTDs are invisible to us because they are part of "impoverished communities." And while some of them are in

---

[2] Mitra, A.K.; Mawson, A.R. Neglected Tropical Diseases: Epidemiology and Global Burden. Trop. Med. Infect. Dis. 2017, 2, 36. https://doi.org/10.3390/tropicalmed2030036

South and Central America, almost none are in North America, Europe, or the rest of the developed world.

The article's author, Dr. Peter Hotez, is a leading expert in NTDs. He writes:

"The scale and extent of the global NTD problem are hard to take in. Almost every destitute person living in sub-Saharan Africa, Southeast Asia, and Latin America is infected with one or more of these diseases. The illnesses last years, decades, and often even a lifetime."[3]

NTDs are not just a medical problem. They are a problem of global deprivation and poverty.

Hotez described how many simple and effective treatments exist for these diseases. But even with the "serious money" committed thus far, he concludes that "these NTD-control programs will need ... $2 billion to $3 billion ... over the next five to seven years."

The scale of this problem is impossible for us to understand from our perspective in the non-destitute, non-tropical world. Simply put, we who live in the developed world neglect these diseases because they don't affect us.

NTDs are primarily caused by parasites. Tropical areas have warm, moist climates that allow parasites to grow in the ground and water. People live off the land, lack clean water supplies, and often go without shoes. The combination of climate and poor economic conditions contributes to the prevalence of NTDs.

Even though the medical causes are easily understood, complex political and social factors stand in the way of solutions. The magnitude of NTDs is so great that experts can only envision a solution that requires billions of dollars and years of coordinated effort.

But what if it didn't?

Zero In On One Billion

Mark wasn't looking for a global problem to solve with ZIOZ. But one line in the article caught his attention:

---

[3] https://www.scientificamerican.com/article/a-plan-to-defeat-neglected-tropical-diseases/

"...(NTDs) can be easily treated, often with a single pill. Various agencies and foundations are collaborating to deliver these drugs, although they have reached only about 10 percent of the population so far."

Cures already existed, yet despite the efforts of some of the world's largest nongovernment organizations (NGOs), they had only reached 10 percent of the people who needed them. The article implied it would cost billions of dollars to reach the rest. How could this be?

Mark was fully absorbed in implementing ZIOZ in the orthopedic clinic during this time. When he learned about NTDs, he didn't fully know what ZIOZ was capable of.

Then, in 2012, God again woke Mark up during the night. But, this time, it was to call him to apply Zero in on Zero to the neglected tropical diseases plaguing over one billion people worldwide.

Mark spent the rest of that year sharing the vision with a small circle of friends and doing initial planning.

The Size of the Problem

On January 1, 2013, Mark founded Sustainable Medical Missions ("Sustainable Med"). His son David, who had previously worked for Habitat for Humanity, was the first employee. Together, they incorporated the organization, created a board, and secured nonprofit status.

One of the first board members was Kathy, the nurse who had helped Mark develop ZIOZ in the orthopedic clinic. "I had never known of NTDs before Mark told me about them," Kathy remembers.

Even after hearing Mark's vision, Kathy had her doubts. "It took us years to get this worked out in one hospital with 10 doctors," she recalls. "There was little to no published research on NTDs, and few doctors knew about them. Applying ZIOZ to NTDs was truly faith in God."

Mark and David spent the rest of 2013 researching and listening. They traveled to Africa to talk with leaders from Kenya and Uganda. These trips soon proved how little they knew about the challenge ahead. But they helped Mark and his team understand the size of the problem.

Neglected and Unknown Diseases

Mark and David were surprised to discover how little information on NTDs existed in the countries afflicted by them. As hard as this was to believe, the explanation made sense when they looked at the healthcare systems.

The doctors and health officials in these countries went to school in Western countries where NTDs did not exist. They knew how to treat diseases that affected Western and more affluent populations but were largely oblivious to the bigger problems plaguing their own people.

These healthcare systems reflected that lack of training and awareness. "They often didn't know what NTDs were," David says. "We knew we had to provide NTD training and explain how ZIOZ could treat infections."

David (far right), Mark (second from right) and Kathy (second from left) at a meeting with pastors and medical leaders in Kenya.

This provided the first insight into why other efforts to address NTDs had failed. Only a few isolated doctors knew about the problem and were working on solutions.

Through God's leading, Mark and David were about to be introduced to one of those doctors.

Short-term and Shortsighted Goals

Dr. David Gordon was trained in Ukraine. He ran what would be considered a clinic by our standards. But it was the only "hospital" for up to 400,000 people in a rural area of Uganda that was a hot spot for neglected tropical diseases. He was trying to meet an overwhelming need with minimal resources. He had received funding to combat NTDs from an NGO in the past, but that funding had run out.

"Dr. Gordon spent two hours telling us about his experience and what we should do to treat NTDs," David recalls. "But when we asked if he was doing what he had told us to do, he said he wasn't!"

Mark and David were stunned and asked him why not. "Well," Dr. Gordon said. "Another NGO came along and paid us to do something else." He could only focus on treating NTDs for a short period of time because, when that funding ran out, he had to abandon what he knew worked to take on a new focus to receive new funding.

Dr. Gordon depended on the NGOs' money to keep the clinic running. However, the NGOs were only there to accomplish short-term goals chosen by experts without the input of those in the area. Once the funding ran out, the NGOs left, and those serving in the clinic had to find another funding source. That meant shifting to another set of short-term objectives decided by someone else.

"These outside programs were never owned by the doctors who were actually doing the work," David states. "When the sponsoring organization left, they stopped doing the program."

This system prevented doctors with the most experience from doing what they knew would help those they were trying to serve. It also explained why there was so little to show for the hundreds of millions of dollars NGOs had spent on treating NTDs.

A Glimmer of Hope

Everything David and Mark had seen on those early trips had shown them one thing: the problem of treating NTDs was much bigger than they had imagined. But instead of being deterred, they were compelled by their faith to continue looking for an answer.

Meeting with Dr. Gordon had given them a glimmer of hope. He knew how to treat NTDs and had made progress while he could focus on them. If there were more doctors like him, and the resource issues could be solved, perhaps there was a way.

Jonathan Burnham training African pastors

Dr. Gordon was a Christian who had been discipled through Burnham Ministries International (BMI), whose vision is to train and equip pastors serving in undeveloped parts of the world, including former Soviet-bloc countries. While working in Ukraine, BMI recognized an opportunity to invest in African medical students like David Gordon.

Mark and his team realized that this connection could potentially lead to a completely different approach to the challenge of treating NTDs.

While this would not be their long-term strategy, it gave them a starting point outside the African medical system.

Sustainable Med Takes Root

Treating the Neglect in NTDs

In talking to Dr. Gordon and others, Mark and David realized that the root of the problem in NTDs was not the disease but neglect. Neglect resulted from people's failure to care for each other.

To treat NTDs, people needed to change. And Mark and David knew the most effective way to change people was through the gospel and biblical discipleship. Their vision was to use biblical discipleship principles to guide medical training, not just add some biblical content to an existing medical approach.

The vision was becoming clear around three components. The organization would be:

- **Sustainable:** They had to succeed with little to no ongoing Western involvement.
- **Medical:** The work would use the ZIOZ method to reduce the number of NTD-related infections to zero.
- **Mission-minded:** The focus would be on lives changed through the gospel.

The Vision Takes Shape

Mark and David began planning in more detail, drawing on a conversation David had previously had with Jonathan Burnham from BMI. David and Mark knew Jonathan from his time as pastor of Hope Church in Mason, Ohio, a suburb of Cincinnati.

Jonathan knew about the needs in Africa from the pastors he had trained. He believed that the illness and suffering in these rural, impoverished communities were the primary obstacle to them hearing the gospel.

Before Sustainable Med was formed, Jonathan had shared a ministry idea with David that involved training pastors to see how the local church could contribute to their local communities' well-being. It was a way to share the gospel more holistically.

"I knew that people with empty stomachs can't have open ears," David recalls. "That conversation with Jonathan confirmed what I had been thinking."

Training pastors on ZIOZ to eradicate NTDs became central to Sustainable Med's mission. These pastors were already part of the communities they needed to reach, and treating NTDs would open doors to share the gospel.

In 2014, Sustainable Med conducted its first three training conferences in Ukraine for about 80 current and future leaders, presenting information on NTDs, ZIOZ, and fundamental truths of Christianity. Twelve attendees were medical students in Ukraine, and the rest were pastors and doctors in Kenya and Uganda.

These were small beginnings. Now, they had to wait and see if their approach would scale treatment for NTDs and create a movement for the gospel.

Scale Down to a "Village Reality"

As Mark thought about what scaling ZIOZ could do, his mind was drawn to the familiar Parable of the Sower from the New Testament. Mark understood that the key was to prepare the soil. That way, you could pray for God to bring the harvest of 30, 60, or 100-fold returns.

Mark and David knew from conversations with people living with the diseases that they were ignorant about the causes. As a result, when the Western NGOs brought in their external programs and imposed them on large populations, those people didn't understand why they needed to do them. Once the program was over, they went back to their old ways.

Mark realized they needed to scale differently if this were to become the movement he envisioned. He had to begin by reducing the problem to a workable size. "He wanted to bring NTDs from a world-scale number to village reality," David said. If they could find solutions that worked at the village level, they could scale to other villages and serve many people.

Mark's heart was drawn to the suffering people and what he could do to improve their lives. This was a very different mindset from those looking to address a rural, third-world problem with Western solutions.

But something else was missing.

From Treatment to Eradication

NGOs examined the size of the problem and tried to scale up Western public health solutions to address it. Mark examined the people affected by NTDs and asked what would improve their individual lives.

This was when his team came upon a key insight: Sustainable Med must focus on eradication, not just treatment. This made sense because a primary goal of ZIOZ when it began in 2008 was preventing the problem, not just treating it after it happened.

The innovation ZIOZ brought to the clinic was to prevent adverse events by looking at the factors before, during, and after. Treatment only looks at the problem after the adverse event has happened.

Prevention was the real power behind the success of ZIOZ in Cincinnati. It broadened the approach to include everyone involved in the patient's care to focus on avoiding problems in the first place. That broader perspective had helped ZIOZ deliver its life-changing results.

Mark described ZIOZ as a "novel, simple process improvement strategy." He believed this strategy could be applied to any problem.

David summarized this change in perspective: "The NGOs failed to scale treatment because the diseases were still being caused by ignorance," David observed. "If you scale a mindset of eradication, the need for treatment diminishes."

The change in perspective from treatment to eradication reframed the problem. But one more piece was needed.

Faith to Solve Problems

Mark wanted to see lives changed by the gospel. As Jonathan had noted, suffering caused by NTDs was the biggest barrier to that happening in these impoverished communities. But the solutions had to come from the people themselves. Otherwise, it would keep them dependent on the Western organizations that funded or treated them.

After a conference, a doctor in Nairobi, Kenya, summarized the challenge: "If you teach the people how to develop themselves, they will change and cause change to the land."

The more the team looked at what hadn't worked, the more they knew genuine faith was part of the answer. NTDs were not only neglected diseases. They were diseases of neglect.

Caring Westerners could alleviate that neglect, but only a relationship with their loving Creator could eliminate it. Knowing God, who made us in his image, allows us to create lasting solutions for our practical problems.

The team developed a simple process that could empower the trainees to develop solutions. This meant those living with NTDs could own the problem and develop ways to address the causes and follow through on the cure.

The training was now ready to empower Christian pastors and medical workers already working in NTD areas with three things:

- Information about the diseases
- The ZIOZ method to identify root causes of disease
- The faith to develop solutions for those problems

The goal was to remove barriers to sharing the hope of the gospel. This was the vision, but would it work?

Small Beginnings

In 2014, Sustainable Med hosted its first in-person training conference in Uganda, Africa. Back then, as today, these introductory conferences are held for small groups of 20-35 people.

Those are small numbers for an organization hoping to care for billions of people. But it's not the number of people reached at the conference that matters. Scale happens in how attendees reproduce themselves afterward.

Attendees come from a mix of backgrounds — about half are medical professionals and half are church- and community-based leaders. This reflects the emphasis on combining medical practice with spiritual and community work. Ideally, two-person teams of medical and non-medical leaders return to each village to share what they have learned.

These conferences have evolved over the years, but their goals remain the same:

1. **Teach new concepts.** Each trainee learns basic NTD information and problem-solving concepts. Everything is designed to be practical and informative. Even the sessions on Christian faith are presented logically, encouraging critical thinking.
2. **Empower.** Trainees are told they can and must develop new and innovative solutions to eradicate NTDs. Much can be learned from the Western medical establishment, but depending on it does not empower those living with NTDs to solve problems and own the solutions.
3. **Build a common language.** Fostering collaboration between medical and faith leaders requires understanding and discussing the material using common terms. Community and faith leaders need to learn basic medical terminology quickly, and medical leaders need to translate what they know into terms that community and faith leaders can understand.

4. **Build relationships and networks.** Existing and new relationships are essential to be effective. The Sustainable Med team knew they could only provide limited follow-up for each trainee. The most valuable resource attendees would take with them would be their relationships with others who were doing the same work under the same conditions.

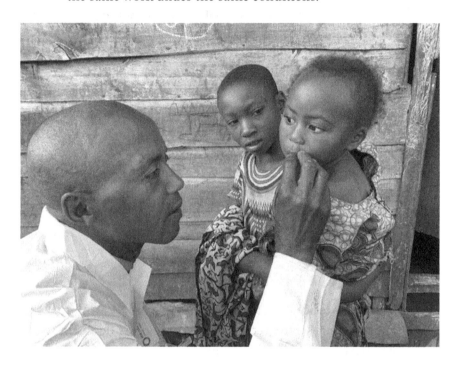

Initial Growth

The 2014 conferences covered a lot of ground in two or three short days, and the value of their approach was soon apparent. The pastors and Christian medical workers were enthusiastic about helping heal the diseases afflicting their communities. They grasped that treating NTDs would create opportunities for sharing the gospel.

David and Mark had seen the failures of the medical system and NGO approaches in addressing the problem of NTDs. Instead of trying to change or compete with these organizations, they had chosen to work through a different network of relationships: the church.

Sustainable Med was building on a movement of biblical discipleship that Jesus' followers had started 2,000 years earlier. Throughout Africa, Christian churches were already established in even remote, neglected villages. By training pastors and church- and community-based leaders who already lived in these communities, Sustainable Med could create a lifetime of impact. And by teaching them to train others, they could extend their reach exponentially.

These two strategies of training those in place and teaching them to train others, fueled by the hope of the gospel, were at the heart of Sustainable Med's vision.

"We didn't go to Africa to tell them what to do," David recalls. "Instead, we let them tell us what they needed." By asking, listening, and following the existing relationships, David and Mark found a group committed to helping those suffering from NTDs.

But how would this approach scale to address the overwhelming problems of NTDs?

5

Key People

The Sustainable Med team had identified the essential processes to bring ZIOZ into the rural villages of Africa. But that was just the beginning. Now, they had to train the doctors, healthcare workers, and pastors on these processes.

How would they decide whom to train? These individuals would need to endure hardship, so they had to be people of faith who could trust God to give them new solutions.

The team developed four criteria for potential trainees. They must:

1. **Be a proclaimed follower of Christ.** Sustainable Med was not an evangelistic program. It was scaling a way to remove the barriers to the gospel created by NTDs. If a trainee was not a believer, they could not fully appreciate this mission.
2. **Have some background in either education or medicine.** The training was rigorous. There was much to learn quickly, and trainees would need to apply that knowledge when they returned home.
3. **Possess a humble and teachable spirit.** Sustainable Med had developed a different approach to NTDs by listening to those who were trying to combat them. This required humility, a quality necessary for all trainees.
4. **Already be working in their communities.** Innovations would come through listening to others. Therefore, trainees

needed to be trusted, credible members of the community, not newcomers.

Each of these criteria was essential, but a track record of community work proved to be the greatest indicator of success. It provided evidence of humility and faith and demonstrated a person's commitment to caring for the most destitute people.

Sustainable Med's ability to scale depended on equipping those whom God had already strategically put in place. Now, they had to see if this would create a movement of community problem-solving.

A Life-Changing Experience

One person who remembers how Sustainable Med's conference changed him is Emmanuel Ndolimana. Raised in Rwanda, Emmanuel was 13 when he and his family fled the country's 1994 genocide. His father was a pastor and church planter who continued his work among refugees in Congo, where the Ndolimana family settled.

From Congo, Emmanuel went to Uganda to receive an English education. He returned to Rwanda in 2001 with a desire to lead a church but realized he needed more theological training. He received a Billy Graham Scholarship to study at Wheaton College outside Chicago, Illinois. There, he met Jonathan Burnham, who connected him to David in 2013.

Emmanuel was an exceptional student. He spoke six languages and would return to Rwanda as part of the country's top 1% of educated individuals. "I used to think I would work for a big organization with a well-paying, white-collar job," he remembers. But God led Emmanuel to a small village to plant a church.

Then, in 2014, Emmanuel attended an early Sustainable Med conference in Uganda. This conference was led by Dr. Lincoln Chirochierwa, who had attended one of the organization's first training conferences while attending medical school in Ukraine.

"The information about NTDs shed the light for me," Emmanuel recalls. "I was planting a church but not caring for the well-being of the people in my community."

He remembers thinking, "I want to take people to heaven, but they are still suffering from these diseases now."

Seeing With New Eyes

After the conference, Emmanuel saw his community with new eyes. "I saw causes of NTDs everywhere," he remembers. "The biggest issue was a lack of clean water." That water was only feet away, but to the villagers, it was unreachable.

"There is a big pipe that goes right through our village that takes clean water to the city," Emmanuel states. "But the government never gave us access to that water, so our people didn't think it was for them, even though their taxes paid for it." They had every right to clean water but lacked the faith to see it as a solution to their problem.

Because of the Sustainable Med training, Emmanuel now had that faith. He contacted a government official and asked that his village be given access to that pipe and the clean water it carried. The official agreed but said the village must provide the reduction valve and pipes necessary to tap into this high-volume supply.

Emmanuel turned to Sustainable Med for help. The organization provided a grant to purchase the valves, pipes, and a storage tank in case of outages. Then, the entire community dug the trench and laid the pipe to the tank, which was placed on the church's land.

Removing Barriers to the Gospel

That experience transformed Emmanuel's perspective. "The community had ownership of the solution, and everyone was part of the celebration," he recalls. "Everyone in the community was welcome to the water, and our church grew from 40 people to over 600 in a few months."

Emmanuel saw something he wanted to be part of. "Sustainable Med was not telling us what to do," he said. "Instead, they were giving us the knowledge that opened our eyes to the problem and helped us develop a solution."

"My experience had been that the solution would come from the West, and the West would be the heroes of the story, but Sustainable Med was completely different," Emmanuel recounts. "The challenge and the solution belong to the people. Sustainable Med stays invisible, and the people see the local church, which is not going away."

Emmanuel wanted to invest his life in this work. On July 1, 2015, he joined the Sustainable Med team as Africa Director. As a result, Emmanuel has regularly hosted training conferences and introduced thousands of people to Sustainable Med's approach.

A Successful Doctor

Lincoln Chirochierwa was the doctor who hosted the Sustainable Med conference in Uganda that Emmanuel attended in 2014. From Emmanuel's perspective, Lincoln was a successful doctor fully committed to the vision of Sustainable Med.

Little did Emmanuel know that Lincoln was confused and asking himself, "What am I doing here?"

When that conference took place, Lincoln was a third-year medical student in Ukraine, anticipating a career in cardiothoracic surgery. Lincoln's family had been regular church attenders while growing up, but his faith was not personal. He stopped attending church for the first two years he lived away from home.

In his third year, Lincoln began to consider his future medical career direction. Around that time, he decided to pursue his faith and ended up in a church connected to Burnham Ministries International. The first Sunday he was there, the pastor walked up to him and said, "I want to invest in you." This began their discipleship relationship.

That pastor was Vitaly Sorokun, and through Jonathan Burnham, Vitaly introduced Lincoln to David and Mark.

Lincoln learned about the vision for Sustainable Med, and David asked him for his ideas. Lincoln told him what he thought would work and what wouldn't work. David ended the meeting by saying, "If anything else comes to mind, let me know."

Mark, Vitaly, and David.

Lincoln was a good student. He planned to go to the U.S. or the United Kingdom to finish his training. Lincoln was interested in what Sustainable Med was planning to do and thought he could support the organization financially once he was a successful doctor.

But something in Lincoln was beginning to change.

The Power of Listening

David's willingness to ask for input had impressed Lincoln. Later that year, Lincoln wrote David a long email with his thoughts on how Sustainable Med's mission would and would not work. That email started a dialogue between Lincoln, David, and Mark.

Then, Lincoln participated in a training conference on ZIOZ for medical students in Ukraine. Mark encouraged Lincoln and the other students to write ZIOZ protocols on NTDs for one of their classes. Lincoln and his roommate wrote most of these protocols and were invited to present them at the upcoming conference in Uganda. Their presentations were to be part of the training sessions.

This invitation made a huge impression on Lincoln. "Never in my experience would students be invited to participate in something like this," he remembers. "We never had the opportunity to be respected and contribute on an equal level."

Mark was a highly accomplished surgeon from the U.S., but he was willing to listen to Lincoln present his material.

"I was confused," he recalls. "This was too much power to give a medical student. I kept asking myself, 'What am I doing here?' But David and Mark kept telling us that our voice mattered."

Lincoln went back to Ukraine, still confused about what his involvement with Sustainable Med should be. He was drawn to what he had experienced through the shared experience of the conference. But he also wanted to pursue medical specialization in the West.

"As I was meeting more people who were part of Sustainable Med, my heart began to change," Lincoln states. "My prayers changed from focusing on what I wanted to become to asking God, 'Where are you leading me?'"

Later that year, Vitaly took Lincoln and other students to a missions conference where Lincoln heard God speaking to him through Isaiah 6:8: "Whom shall I send, and who will go for us?"

Lincoln's heart responded with the rest of that verse. "Here I am! Send me."

6

Supporting a Movement

Scaling Sustainability

Sustainable Med was finding the right people to train, and God was connecting them to the key individuals who would help them scale their training to support a movement for the gospel.

But they still had to solve the problem of sustaining this work at scale. They would not follow the usual NGO playbook and use their initial success to raise more money. Instead, they trusted God to provide funds they could invest in sustainability.

In 2015, Sustainable Med began offering education scholarships and innovation grants to people who identified solutions to systemic problems in their communities.

Some of these short-term funds are used for infrastructure projects, such as digging wells to provide a safe water source. Others helped establish profitable businesses that provide services that are missing in these communities. Once these businesses are established, they can financially support ongoing ZIOZ training in that region.

These grants continue to fuel Sustainable Med's efforts to scale. By choosing opportunities that can become self-sustaining, the team is ensuring the work continues without ongoing support from the West.

Back in the states, Doug Walouke was Sustainable Med's treasurer and managed the funds for these innovation grants. "We need to get ready for the growth that's coming," Doug remembers thinking. "The requests for grants are pouring in."

Leaders of Excellence

Sustainable Med had developed training around the medical and missions components of their vision. It also invested in sustainability by funding self-sustaining businesses.

But to support a movement, they would have to invest in a new generation of leaders who could own the vision. These would be "Leaders of Excellence."

Mark had already developed leadership for Sustainable Med through his son, David. The organization had invested in leadership in Africa, choosing to keep their U.S.-based staff to a minimum.

It was time to give more ownership to the people who had demonstrated they could scale the ZIOZ approach in the areas where they lived and served.

As the Sustainable Med team stayed in contact with the trainees, they saw some take it to another level by investing in others. "We saw some were doing it well, following a high standard," Emmanuel states. "They were starting to invest in others, so we identified them as ambassadors of what we are about."

Sustainable Med's leadership began investing in these individuals by inviting them to an advanced training conference, the first of which was held in 2016.

These advanced conferences reviewed material and core concepts from the first conference but focused most on community building. Participants broke into small groups to analyze the factors before, during, and after the problem facing their home community, using ZIOZ to help refine a solution.

These discussions were transformative for many who attended the advanced training. Those who continued to train others in ZIOZ were invited to become Leaders of Excellence.

Community Impact

Today, Leaders of Excellence are training other people at an exponential rate. As they share ideas and stories with each other, Sustainable Med leaders hear about more and more effective solutions.

Sustainable Med continues to strategically support leaders who demonstrate ownership and potential. "These projects are their projects and not that of Sustainable Med," David asserts. "We have guidelines, but our partners get to decide the diseases they treat and how to implement their projects."

To be eligible for future funding, leaders must submit reports to verify each project's effectiveness. These reports include pre- and post-project testing for disease rates. They also report on local contributions, including the volunteer labor that goes into the project.

"These reports allow us to track the effect of the training and the funds," David states. "Often, the community's investment is 15 to 20 times more than what they received, considering the value of the volunteer labor." This underscores the community's active role and ownership.

The impact on these communities has been nothing short of transformative. The combination of using ZIOZ to combat NTDs and sharing God's love through the gospel has been a catalyst for other changes, sparking a wave of hope and optimism.

This hope and optimism provide the energy that fuels a movement. Community members who have never been trained in ZIOZ are asking what they can do to help alleviate the suffering around them.

Hope in the Gospel

Many pastors have caught a vision for how their communities can be transformed through this process, further fueling hope and optimism.

Channeling innovation through the local church to serve the community has helped churches grow quickly. "Many of these churches were small groups of 30 people meeting under a mango tree," David says. "Now they are 200, 300 people or more."

Sustainable Med provides funding to help these church communities create multipurpose buildings for both worship and learning. The organization's funds pay for supplies that are not available locally, such as roofing, nails, and trusses.

These buildings, known as Life Centers, offer training on ZIOZ and hygiene and even house Christian schools. They are a community resource where people can experience the transformative power of God's work through Sustainable Med.

Community Transformation

Etienne Turimumahoro is one pastor who has used Sustainable Med training and resources to transform his remote village in Rwanda. In 2015, his community was near the bottom of the country in every metric including health, literacy, and economic prosperity.

Etienne was invited to a Sustainable Med training conference. He took the ZIOZ process home and began developing solutions with his community. When they first learned about NTDs, residents did not even have soap to wash their hands, so they used sand instead.

Etienne empowered the community with his efforts to reduce NTDs. He even got the commander of the local army regiment to send his men to help dig latrines.

The church began to grow, and Etienne applied for funds to build a Life Center. As the people in his community were healed of NTDs, they had the energy to do other work. He then began to work to improve the schools and connected to another NGO to provide sewing machines and teach the women in his community how to use them. This raised the community's economic prosperity.

In 2021, the government recognized this village as the top community across every metric for the entire nation of Rwanda.

The Hands and Feet of Jesus

Doug Walouke traveled to Africa in 2019 and vividly remembers visiting Etienne's village on a missions trip with David and Mark. "I was on the back of Etienne's motorcycle," Doug recalls. "A bridge had washed out, and the others in my group needed to fix it before the cars could get across." So, Doug and Etienne arrived in the village first.

As they approached, the air was filled with joyous singing. "People were lining the road, dancing and clapping," he remembers. "No one spoke English, but everyone wanted to hug me and shake my hand, and I would high-five with kids."

Doug Greeting Villagers in Rwanda

For about half an hour, Doug was the center of this incredible outpouring of joy and gratitude. "All I could do was receive their overwhelming thankfulness," Doug says. "All I had done was show up."

Once everyone arrived in the village, they got down to the work they had come to do. Later in the day, however, Doug had a chance to tell them what he had experienced. "Mark said to me, 'Doug, you just represented the hands and feet of Jesus. That's what they were celebrating.'"

That moment captured Mark's vision for Sustainable Med: bringing together medicine and the gospel. Being the hands and feet of Jesus meant bringing healing from NTDs to this remote village and seeing people lift themselves out of poverty and despair into health and joy.

A Movement Started

This was the beginning of the movement God had placed on Mark's heart in 2013. The 2024 data speaks for itself.

In 10 years, Sustainable Medical Missions has:

- Trained over 60,000 community healthcare workers and local pastors
- Impacted over four million people suffering from NTDs
- At a cumulative cost of less than $3 million

This is a small start compared to Dr. Hoetz's prediction that $2-3 billion is needed to treat one billion people. But the exponential effect of scale and the movement it creates are the real cause for hope.

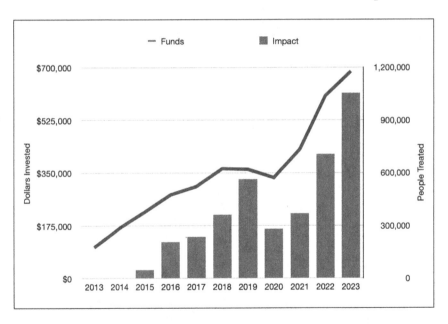

Dr. Hoetz had predicted it that the NGOs approach would cost $2-3 per person to treat the 1 billion people with NTDs. But Sustainable Med was impacting people for less than 60 cents per person, less than a third of the cost of the NGOs!

In addition, the ongoing effect of empowering local leaders means the cost continues to go down as the impact increases. This impact does not end when the funding goes away. Rather, by funding self-sustaining businesses, the impact increases while the need for funding stops.

"We may be less than five years away from Rwanda being completely self-sustaining and continuing their rates of NTD eradication," David states. "That would be the fulfillment of our vision."

7

A Movement for the Gospel

Sustainable Med and The Gospel

God gave Mark a solution in ZIOZ that would change millions of lives. It changed hospitals' approach to surgical care in the world's most advanced health systems. But ZIOZ did not change the hearts of those providing surgical care.

In impoverished communities suffering from neglect, ZIOZ saved lives through community-based solutions. But the content presented by Sustainable Med on its own could not address the neglect experienced by those living with NTDs.

Mark's reason for scaling ZIOZ through Sustainable Med was to remove the barriers to the gospel created by NTDs. His team discovered that Christians who were already serving these communities were best suited to this task.

As a result, churches are growing. Pastors have gained credibility in their communities, which has opened doors for the gospel. Muslim communities have invited Sustainable Med to teach ZIOZ and to share the gospel.

God is using the scale of ZIOZ to share the good news of Jesus Christ with others.

Stewards of Influence

God is also using Sustainable Med to further empower those already in positions of influence. One such person is Dr. Stephen Mwatha.

Stephen was raised in a Christian home in Kenya and attended medical school in Ukraine, where he met Pastor Vitaly. After his training, Stephen returned to Kenya and took a position in a rural hospital.

He was also serving with the Kenyan Ministry of Health in the division that treated NTDs. He was monitoring a drug treatment program similar to one that the NGOs run.

"We noticed that infection rates went back up after the programs stopped," Stephen states. "We realized we needed to communicate a behavior change that would help prevent and avoid infection."

In 2012, Pastor Vitaly called Stephen and asked him to meet with Mark and David, who were coming to Africa. When the men met, Stephen recognized that the ZIOZ approach would be effective in his strategy.

"ZIOZ was asking what happens before, during, and after, which includes helping people change their behavior," he states. Stephen's team saw how they could achieve their objectives by combining the ZIOZ approach with their program.

Sustainable Med was influencing the medical system in Kenya. But more influence was still to come.

Growing Influence

Stephen joined the Sustainable Med board in 2020 to deepen the relationship between Sustainable Med and the Kenyan Ministry of Health.

This allowed Stephen to see more of the data that Sustainable Med was collecting from its partners and identify opportunities to publish some of it as medical research. Stephen recognized that God had placed him in a strategic position to influence other leaders.

Stephen was focused on a particular NTD called trachoma, which is the leading cause of blindness in the world and a significant issue in Kenya and the surrounding countries.

Sustainable Med started a project in 2020 that taught community health volunteers how to test for trachoma. Diagnosing trachoma in the early stages of the disease is important because early treatment can prevent blindness without surgery.

The Sustainable Med program proved to be effective. "Based on the data from Sustainable Med, the Kenyan Ministry of Health decided to roll out the testing approach at a national level," Stephen recalls.

Dr. Stephen Mwatha presenting at a 2024 conference.

Kenya has since become a leader in treating trachoma in Africa. The Kenyan Ministry of Health has built relationships with surrounding countries to help eradicate the disease and partnered with other NGOs to fund the work.

Through their combined efforts, millions of people are keeping their sight, dramatically improving their quality of life.

Scaling Influence for The Gospel

Stephen's relationship with Sustainable Med had increased his influence inside the Kenyan Ministry of Health and in the surrounding countries. However, Stephen sees an even greater way Sustainable Med is scaling influence for the gospel.

"The unique component of Sustainable Med is the integration of medical work and pastors," he states. "They equip pastors to become advocates of health." This integration helps pastors become proactive in their communities, which creates more opportunities for them to share the gospel.

"In Kenya, there is a lot of respect for ministers," Stephen explains. "They are key people for sharing information because they are trusted in the community."

Stephen recognized how the Sustainable Med approach also gives pastors an advantage. "By communicating the information, pastors can show compassion for those suffering from NTDs," Stephen explains. "People see them as compassionate leaders, and they have a better understanding of the problems facing their communities."

Stephen helped identify pastors in Kenya who would be interested in this type of work. He encouraged each of them to identify a healthcare worker to closely partner with. Together, they could deploy various programs to eradicate NTDs.

Because pastors are respected, their involvement in eradicating NTDs helps the community trust the healthcare workers. And the healthcare workers help pastors be aware of the suffering of their people and offer them the healing that ZIOZ can bring.

These relationships represent real savings for the healthcare system, which gets the attention of government officials. "We've seen that every dollar spent on prevention saves eight to sixteen dollars to treat the disease," Stephen remarks.

These partnerships are key to the scaling influence of these spiritual leaders. By working together, pastors and medical workers are creating a movement for the gospel.

But it's not just doctors, healthcare workers, and government leaders that God is using.

The Janitor and Pumpkin Seeds

Henry Mutebi was a young Christian boy working as a janitor in a rural clinic in an impoverished area of Rwanda. A Sustainable Med conference was being offered in the region, and Henry was invited to go.

"He didn't even know why he was there," remembers Lincoln, but learning about NTDs and ZIOZ caught Henry's attention. "He applied for a scholarship to become a lab assistant," Lincoln continues. "Soon, he was experimenting with a lot of innovation."

Henry lived in a region with high rates of ascariasis, a type of roundworm infection. These parasites use the body as a host to mature from larvae or eggs to adult worms. Adult worms, which reproduce, can be more than 12 inches long. Ascariasis is the most common NTD in the world, affecting nearly 100 million people worldwide.

Henry noticed that some of the pigs in the area didn't have the parasites, but he couldn't explain why. He applied the ZIOZ process and noticed that the parasite-free pigs were fed pumpkin seeds. Pumpkins were a common food source, but the seeds were considered garbage that some people fed to their pigs.

As Henry continued to engage his community in the problem, he was reminded that his grandmother had made tea with pumpkin seeds to treat his stomach aches as a child. This gave Henry the idea to do an experimental project using pumpkin seed tea to treat this NTD. He applied for a grant from Sustainable Med and set to work.

A Cure From Garbage

The results of Henry's study were remarkable. Henry found that pumpkin seed tea is 90% effective in treating the most common NTD in the world! A pill is available to treat ascariasis, but it is not always accessible. But a janitor who became a lab assistant had discovered a cure in something considered garbage!

Stephen learned about Henry's project and is helping him prepare a research paper for publication. "While doing our research, we found others who had used pumpkin seeds for deworming animals," Stephen states. "That confirmed our results."

Henry was just getting started. He has since used ZIOZ to address the problem of infant mortality due to the need for blood transfusions after birth.

"Look who is God raising up to do his work," Lincoln says about Henry. "This is a great African innovation story!"

God Has Used ZIOZ in Big Ways

Henry's story about the pumpkin seeds illustrates what God can accomplish through a janitor in a rural hospital in Africa. This remarkable young man is showing the world the scientific mind God gave him, and Sustainable Med is helping make his amazing work possible.

Sustainable Med strategically chose to invest in Henry and other Christ-followers. That meant equipping them with information on NTDs and ZIOZ. In doing so, they could be more effective at what they were already doing and see the benefits of working together toward a shared goal.

Sustainable Med has scaled by giving ownership to the people it trains. In the process, they have created a movement.

"We are hearing back from people who have taken our training into areas we could never go," David exclaims. "The largest church denomination in Africa has invited us to train their pastors, all because someone started using ZIOZ in their community."

"Sustainable Med is all small things," Kathy said. "But God has used it in big ways."

God continues to use Sustainable Med in big ways, but how can its experience apply to other forms of scale to create movements?

To answer that, we must now turn to the question: What is scale?

PART 2

What Is Scale?

Why Scale?

Scale is the phenomenon of exponential growth.

Humans have known principles of growth for a long time, dating back to ancient times. Any empire that grew to dominate its surroundings discovered and applied these principles.

But the pace and the means of growth have increased exponentially in the last few decades. This exponential growth — growth by multiplication, not mere addition—is what we mean by scale. Businesses learned to multiply growth, which is why scale now dominates conversations in the business world.

But scale didn't start with business.

Scale has been part of God's redemptive purpose from the beginning. Scale was in God's mandate to the man and woman he created in his image. It's visible through the Bible's stories, particularly in the spread of the church in Acts. Whenever a church talks about its discipleship mission, it is talking about scale.

Until the industrial era, scale moved very slowly. We couldn't see it until we looked back over the arc of history. But the pace of growth has dramatically changed in our digital world. Now scale vies for our attention on every connected device, telling us what's trending and suggesting what we need to know, creating the fear we will miss out on the next big thing.

Scale has accomplished much good. We use scale for sanitation, food supplies, and medical care, which save, improve, and prolong lives. But scale also can destroy. Lives have been lost, or their quality degraded due to mechanized warfare, pollution, and the spread of disease.

Scale that is controlled and directed toward serving others is a means to create much good. Scale that is uncontrolled or pointed towards a self-serving purpose is a means to cause much harm.

We cannot avoid scale, nor would we want to.

Seeing Scale

Scale is all around us. It is already happening in countless ways we are not aware of.

The fact that you are reading these words is the result of scale. This book could not have happened without Gutenberg's press, mass publication, online marketing, or digital distribution. Each of those developments is an outworking of scale.

Scale often fascinates us while it is new, then quickly becomes expected and mundane. How many gadgets do you have that quickly became obsolete? How many apps are on your phone that you've not opened in months?

Scale accounts for the physical goods that fill our lives. Look around the room you are in. How many of the items you see were mass-produced? Scale in manufacturing has become so commonplace that it has elevated the status of non-manufactured things to art or craft.

Scale changes what we value. Because of scale, we expect things to cost less, making the things that haven't scaled either obsolete or more valuable.

This change in value has redefined business. Many businesses have found a place in a global supply chain driven by economies of scale. Others have found a way to remain exclusive.

Either way, we must reckon with scale.

Another Story of Scale

The business world took notice when Facebook acquired Instagram in 2012 for $1 billion. That was an incredible amount of money for an app that let you take and share pictures, something you could already do with a smartphone.

But Instagram had something different. In addition to its nostalgic filters, Instagram made it easy to interact with your social circle. As a result, smartphone users were downloading Instagram and making it their social media hub.

Instagram's growth on smartphones got the attention of Mark Zuckerberg, Facebook's founder and CEO. Facebook had scaled to be the dominant social media platform on personal computers, but in 2011, it had not yet begun moving to mobile phones. Zuckerberg realized that an app like Instagram could quickly replace Facebook. His only option was to buy, copy, or kill such a competitor.

Before Facebook's offer, a venture capital firm had signed a deal to invest $50 million in Instagram. The firm expected Instagram to one day be worth $500 million, 10 times its current size. Then, Mark Zuckerberg called and doubled that amount in his famous $1 billion offer.

Facebook was weeks away from its IPO, which they expected would value Facebook at $90 billion. Facebook had taken eight years to reach this point. That rate of growth was unprecedented—until Facebook purchased Instagram.

Below is a quick timeline of this scale:

- Instagram started as an idea in 2009.
- In 2010, it raised $500,000 and grew to one million daily users.
- In September 2011, it had 10 million users.
- In April 2012, it raised $50 million. Four days later, it sold to Facebook for $1 billion.
- By the end of April 2012, Instagram had 50 million users.
- In early 2013, it had 100 million users.
- By 2019, 1 billion people were using Instagram.

Instagram went from an idea to a valuation of $1 billion in two years (2010 to 2012) and passed 2 billion users in 2024. That was a new dimension of scale.

Production and Money in Scale

Instagram illustrates a more technical definition of scale, which is the ability for something to grow larger or increase in number in a way that does not require significantly more resources.

In manufacturing, scale is measured by two key drivers: production and money. These are the basis of the mechanical process of creating and selling physical products. However, as Instagram demonstrates, digital production differs from physical production.

Creating the computer or smartphone and the servers that power these services still requires a physical process. However, once a digital service is launched, adding more users takes minimal physical investment.

Once users have the app, the goal is to get them to spend more time on it measured by user engagement, which is then used to sell advertising. Digital technology has taken scale to a whole new level, and several of the world's most valuable companies are always tech companies.

Scaling Communication

Written communication is another example of scale. It has always taken some effort to write a letter to someone. The typewriter helped speed up the physical effort; secretaries could transcribe as quickly as someone spoke. Carbon paper created two copies simultaneously.

But until the photocopier, and then digital printers, each copy or two had to be typed by a person. That's why companies employed rooms full of women to work on typewriters. Still, those letters or documents had to be sent, delivered, and filed by hand.

Contrast that to sending an email today. Composing an email still requires some effort, but then everything changes. You enter the email address and hit send, and it takes almost no effort to add a second or third person, or group of people, to that email. Email is a technology that easily allows us to scale our written communication. That's why spam email is such an annoyance!

This illustrates how scale creates value by making things cost less. But scale has also driven down the value of written communication overall. How many unread emails do you have, and how much junk arrives in your physical mailbox?

That said, scale does not always drive the value of something down. If it did, we could never apply scale to something inherently good.

The Value of Scale

The companies I've referenced are defined by their financial value, among other things. When we quantify a big problem, we sometimes do so by defining what it will cost to solve.

Money, in its stand-in role, reveals our desires and needs. It is not the end goal but a means to acquire, retain, or regulate what we truly value. As we all know, money cannot purchase happiness or love. It's merely a tool that reflects our pursuit of these intangible aspects of life.

Money reveals much about scale because it reveals much about us. However, this is also the limitation of using money to understand scale. Since money and scale are linked, scale reveals what we desire. For something to scale, a group of people must want it. Marketers help define those groups by linking products and services to the intangible things that matter to us.

That group identification can be trivial, such as how a particular consumer good expresses our sense of style. Or it can be historically significant, such as how social media facilitates political uprisings.

This is often the point where scale becomes a movement. Scale makes something possible that was before unobtainable. Having that thing identifies us with a group that represents what we value.

Knowing we want something others want emboldens us to pursue it.

A Biblical Framework
for Scale

Assessing Scale

Scale reveals our behavior and influences our understanding of who we are and where we belong. The business perspective fails to explain how scale moves into these intangible areas of human experience. Without that understanding, we cannot assess how God can use scale.

To scale in a way that cares for people, we must assess scale with categories traditionally defined by faith. We need a way to assess scale's impact on human beings.

John A. List is an economist who studied scale at Uber and other fast-scaling technology companies. He states people are "inherently unscalable" because they possess unique skills.[4*]

List advises profit-driven companies to scale products and services that don't require unique skills. For example, Uber scaled the availability of cars and drivers. In this sense, scale emphasizes the basic human abilities that are interchangeable and denies the differences that make us individuals.

---

[4] *List, John A. The Voltage Effect Pg. 75.

This advice reveals the tension between an economic view of scale and our Christian faith. The Bible teaches us we are all uniquely valuable because we have been created by God. He made each of us to have a relationship with him and others. Removing that uniqueness denies God's purpose for his creation.

From this narrow view, scale would always be against God's purposes. But more broadly, scale meets many of our physical needs, freeing us to work on our relationships with God and others.

Scale can meet our basic needs. But to use scale beyond that, we must consider our greatest need, which is a relationship with God to overcome the effect of our sin.

God's Redemptive Purpose

God created the world as an expression of his character. He made man and woman specifically in his image, which included the ability to choose. While they chose to obey, God's universal presence was available to them in a very personal, intimate way.

But Adam and Eve chose against God when they were tempted to take the fruit God forbade them to eat. When they did so, they broke their relationship with God and with God's creation. Sin entered the world and has separated us from God and each other ever since.

We are all corrupted by sin, so we all choose against God. The punishment for that choice is eternal separation from God, which is spiritual death. But God didn't leave us there.

God sent his Son, Jesus, into the world. Jesus was both God and man. He never rebelled against God and was obedient even to the point of dying in our place. But Jesus didn't stay dead. God accepted his death for our sins and raised Jesus back to life.

We can trust in Jesus's death as the payment for our sins and be restored in our relationship with God and his creation. Anyone who accepts God's salvation in Jesus can choose to live for God instead of themselves each day and in every situation.

This is the unchanging truth of the Gospel. God is reconciling us to him and reconciling the world through us. However, we still live with the tension of being separated from God by our sin while he draws us to him through his Son.

We can try to fill our need for connection through the things we own and the groups we belong to, and scale makes that easier to do. But God wants to fill our need for connection through a restored relationship with him.

This is his redemptive purpose. So where does scale fit with that?

The Basic Unit of Scale

Measuring scale by products (or the users of those products) and money diminishes the value of our uniqueness and the relationships we build with others. In this form, scale tempts us away from God's purpose and who we were created to be.

In contrast, God's redemptive purpose requires that we see human beings as the basic unit of scale.

Scripture teaches that while all creation reflects God's character, only man and woman are created in his image. Only humans possess a spiritual soul that will live in heaven or hell for eternity, making people the most valuable thing in creation.

We are called to share in the redemptive work of restoring God's image in us through a relationship with him. Even though God's image in us is darkened by sin, he empowers us to respond to the need others have to be reconciled to him.

To assess scale from a biblical perspective, we must evaluate its impact on human beings. Whether scale is good or bad is determined by whether it supports this biblical purpose of redemption.

We are created to be relational, but scale makes things impersonal. These different purposes create a tension we can represent with this line.

Impersonal ◄─────────────────────────► Relational

But we are not just users of the end result of scale. We also participate in scale, often unknowingly.

Are People Scalable?

From a biblical perspective, people have the highest value, so we must assess the effects of scale based on how it impacts people. That includes how scale affects us as we participate in it.

On one hand, people are scalable in that we reproduce and tend to dominate any environment in which we live. All humans are also very sophisticated machines that can do various tasks in various conditions. Those interchangeable skills make them a highly scalable unit of economic production.

On the other hand, individuals are not scalable because no two humans are exactly alike. We share humanity's inherent abilities and limitations, but we must also come to terms with our own particular abilities and limitations.

Each person has an individual and meaningful perspective on the world. This sense of value takes on greater significance if you believe we are an expression of an infinite Creator and not just the product of random selection.

Our individuality creates a tension with scale over what is valuable about humanity. We are created as individuals, but scale emphasizes what is interchangeable.

These different values create a second tension we can represent by another line.

Interchangeable ◀──────────────────────────▶ Individual

If we can tap into this human potential, the possibilities for scale are much greater. But when is it beneficial to see humans based on their common characteristics?

The Redemptive Framework

This biblical understanding of people reveals two tensions with scale. These two lines can be arranged into a two-by-two framework, with the impersonal, relational tension as the X axis and the interchangeable, individual tension as the Y axis.

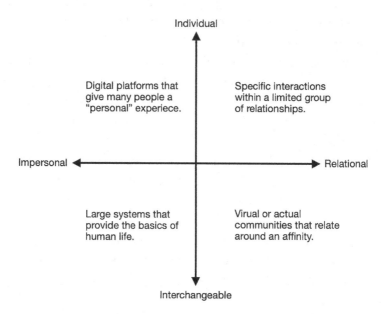

We've now divided the effects of scale into four quadrants.

The Impersonal/Interchangeable Quadrant

The lower left is where scale has helped with the basics of human life. Think of products and services that we see as basic rights, such as food, water, electricity, and, more recently, internet access. While not free, these should be equally available regardless of who you are. Disparities violate our sense of justice.

In our Christian faith, this quadrant might represent the physical buildings where Christians gather to worship. Those buildings require electricity and plumbing, and they are impersonal and interchangeable in that they can be used for other activities. Any suitable space can be used as a place of worship.

The Impersonal/Individual Quadrant

The top left moves into more personalized services, such as fast-scaling digital platforms like Facebook, Instagram, Netflix, and Google, with their billions of users. Yet each person experiences an individual combination of items in their "feed" based on their previous choices.

In the Christian world, this quadrant could encompass large, event-styled services and conferences. You can gather with thousands of people, but sound and video technology create the impression you are face-to-face with the presenter on stage. A shared liturgy also falls into this quadrant, in that millions of people in thousands of congregations recite the same words and read the same scriptures in a given week.

The Interchangeable/Relational Quadrant

The lower right represents a different type of shared experience. This describes the communities or groups you can join online or in person. You may never individually interact with some of these people, but you can relate to them at a certain basic level because of what you have in common. Many such affinity groups exist, and you can easily leave one and join another.

This quadrant could include a community group or Bible study you join in a church. These groups may use mass-produced curriculum; you can interact with group members around the themes of the study without going much deeper. Many churches work to make these groups interchangeable to fit their attendees' busy schedules.

The Individual/Relational Quadrant

The top right is the most antithetical to scale. These are things that are individual to us and are specifically relational. My text conversations with family and friends may use an interchangeable and impersonal service, but the interactions are specific to them. And, with rare exceptions, they are only valuable to the people involved.

The Christian parallel would be one-on-one discipleship relationships or fellowship groups of three or four people. These relationships require commitment and a willingness to forgo other activities. The benefits are often slower to realize, but once experienced, they cannot be easily replicated.

Using the Framework

The Redemptive Framework helps us assess how scale impacts people. The gospel tells us that our greatest need is a relationship with our loving Creator. The things closest to that can be found at the top right.

The elements represented by the other quadrants are not wrong in themselves, and each plays a role in getting us to that individual, relational experience that reflects what God created us to have.

The Movement of Scale

This Redemptive Scale diagram helps simplify the tensions between an economic view of scale and our Christian faith. But our experience of scale has become more complex in the digital age. It has brought many benefits and improvements to life but has also exacerbated some of our spiritual problems.

In the past, for example, when we encountered a problem with a system, such as a government bureaucracy or a bank, we could expect to find a person to help us. People ran and maintained these systems, and making your appeal to the person in the right position could change things.

When plotted on the redemptive framework, our interaction with scale was limited to either the lower left impersonal/interchangeable quadrant or the top right individual/relational quadrant. Our experience with the top left impersonal/individual quadrant was mostly nonexistent. And our communities in the bottom right interchangeable/relational quadrant were personal and centered around existing institutions, such as neighborhood, church, or school.

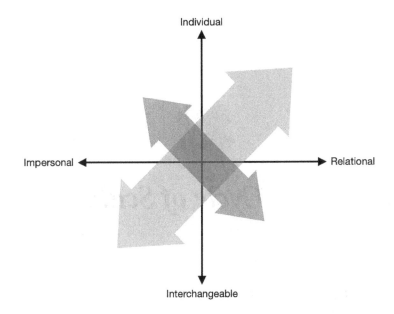

The digital revolution has made these systems more efficient and plentiful, but that has come at the cost of personal interaction. You can now log on to your bank, utility, or countless other accounts directly, which is good when everything works. If it doesn't, you may have to sit on hold for a long time to speak to someone who can change something on your behalf.

We've learned that adapting our behavior to the system is easier than adapting the system to our needs. In this way, scale is moving us away from relating to others and so works against the vision of humanity given to us in Scripture.

In truth, the impact of scale is more complex than this simplistic view allows. To appreciate that complexity, we need to see how scale moves. This will help us understand how it causes harm and how it can create movements for good.

The Cycle of Scale

Scaling Distorted Identities

Instagram is an example of scale's potentially harmful effects.

Instagram's founders had a system to create scale. That system was interchangeable and impersonal, making it easy to use. But users chose Instagram because it provided an individual way to express their view of the world to those in their social circle.

Instagram's scale did shape a culture, but that culture did not promote a biblical understanding of what makes us valuable. In particular, Instagram did not help teenage girls find community by developing relationships with those around them.[5][*]

Instead, Instagram overemphasized physical appearance, so its culture distorted the sense of identity of many who used it. Instagram allowed users to modify their appearance to be more ideal, conveying that those who did not fit this "ideal" were not attractive and therefore were not valuable. As a result, users become part of virtual communities formed by mimicking social influencers on Instagram.

---

[5] [*] This has been written about in numerous books and articles. One excellent sources is *The Anxious Generation: How the Great Rewiring of Childhood Is Causing an Epidemic of Mental Illness*, by Jonathan Haidt.

As more and more users followed those influencers, they skewed the algorithms that populated users' feeds. As a result, the system scaled a looks-based, unhealthy view of identity.

The financial success of monetizing Instagram created a new category of visual social media and the role of professional influencers. This harmful community informed the systems behind multiple image- or video-based apps that have exacerbated these harmful effects.

Instagram went through many iterations before Facebook bought it, and it continues to change. But this progression captures the overall development of its scale, and how it contributed to a destructive cultural movement in social media.

The Cycle of Scale

Our experience of scale is no longer limited between the impersonal/ interchangeable and the individual/relational. We now experience scale in a cycle.

I call this the Cycle of Scale and have broken it down into five basic steps:

1. Systems Create Scale
2. Scale Shapes Culture
3. Culture Forms Identity
4. Identity Becomes Community
5. Communities Inform Systems

These steps overlay the redemptive framework like this:

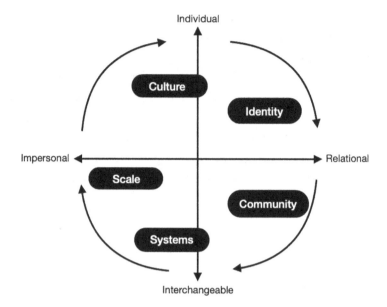

By definition, systems are interchangeable. The foundation of the digital revolution was the invention of hardware that could function on the simplest code possible: off or on, or 1 or 0. That most basic of languages made possible a dizzying variety of digital products and services.

Scale, as we have seen, is impersonal. But if the product or service is not useful to an individual, people won't choose it, and it won't scale. The more a person feels that product or service individually expresses who they are, the more they will invest in it.

When a significant group of people chooses something, it becomes part of our culture. Because we chose it, it feels individual to us, even though countless others have made the same choice. That product or service has become part of how we understand and express ourselves.

When a product or service reflects who we are, it becomes part of our identity. Our individual experience of its value means someone else must appreciate that value to understand and relate to us.

As that product or service limits to whom we relate, we begin to form communities with people who agree on its value. These communities make our experiences interchangeable with others by allowing us to share our experiences with those who think and feel as we do.

The shared experiences inside that community reinforce our sense of ownership. This gives us a combined voice in shaping how the interchangeable system is maintained or changed.

This completed process gives rise to another rotation of the cycle. Now, a new system can arise based on the changes suggested by the community of early adopters.

Let's look at each of these steps in light of how Zero in on Zero scaled.

1. Systems Create Scale

Zero in on Zero is a system people can use to eliminate adverse orthopedic surgery events and address challenges people living with NTDs face.

ZIOZ scaled in the joint replacement surgery setting because orthopedic surgery scaled first. Hip and knee replacements went from being non-existent to widely available in less than 100 years. As interchangeable procedures and tools made this complicated surgery more available, more and more people wanted the benefits it brought.

A system is a group of processes that work together to accomplish something in a more efficient or exponential way.

But, adverse events scaled along with the procedures themselves. One of the 10 adverse events Mark and Kathy set out to eliminate was surgical site infections, which despite billions of dollars spent on treatment, still cost thousands of lives each year.

Many considered these adverse events as an acceptable risk, believing the good done by the surgery outweighed the harm caused by this adverse event.

Joint replacement had become a system that scaled, but that system was impersonal. It prioritized the overall statistical likelihood of an adverse event, not each patient's individual experience.

2. Scale Shapes Culture

Culture is often used to describe the many intangible experiences and interactions in a group. However, culture has a broader function that relates to scale.

Culture gives us shared categories to understand ourselves and explain who we are to others.

Culture is part of any situation in which we interact with others. That includes our work, where culture is often communicated through professional training or expectations. The values and priorities leaders set help shape an organization's culture.

The medical system that trained doctors and cared for patients shaped the culture in the orthopedic clinic where Mark and Kathy were implementing ZIOZ. In this culture, surgeons are solely responsible for their patients' well-being. This makes them the authority on the care they provide and contributes to the culture of physician invulnerability.

This medical culture meant surgeons did not have to collaborate with each other, and only the surgeons would have input on how they cared for their patients. This culture emphasized each doctor's individual skills but made it difficult for them to see the impact their decisions were having on the patient population as a whole.

By contrast, the point of ZIOZ was to collectively find the best procedures by getting input from everyone who interacted with a patient before, during, and after the procedure.

3. Culture Forms Identity

Culture forms our identities through the shared categories we use to understand and explain ourselves to others. Culture is the outside-in perspective, whereas identity is the inside-out perspective.

Our identity is how we see ourselves and explain ourselves to others within the various cultures and communities in which we interact.

Mark was a respected orthopedic surgeon. But he was also a deeply committed Christ-follower. He understood and experienced the gospel, and it deeply affected his understanding of who he was. Kathy was also a believer, and her faith had been a key reason why Mark chose her to work with him on ZIOZ.

Mark's identity was formed by both the medical culture and a culture shaped by his faith. He was a surgeon, so he understood the demands of the medical system. But as a believer, he saw each person as individually created in God's image.

This made Mark particularly relational with his patients and prompted him to ask God for wisdom and compassion in caring for them. He was known to pray with his patients before surgery, even if they did not share his beliefs. And his identity also influenced how he worked with others in the clinic.

For Mark, each person in the clinic had an individual value that must be respected. This included the doctors, nurses, patients, and everyone else involved in the patient's care. Mark believed that everyone had a valuable contribution to make.

Mark was gracious and relational. He constantly sought ways to acknowledge others' contributions to his practice and identify with his patients in their suffering.

4. Identity Becomes Community

The surgeons in the orthopedic clinic participated in ZIOZ, but their individual sense of identity kept many of them from buying in. Orthopedic surgery nurses, however, did buy in. The culture ZIOZ was creating was shaping their identities.

Mark's goals and approach in ZIOZ deeply resonated with how nurses saw themselves as caring medical professionals. These nurses were becoming a community of care for their patients.

Community forms when we identify with a group, choosing to give up aspects of our individual identities.

The orthopedic nursing team cared for all of the surgeons' patients while they were in the hospital. Each surgical nurse worked with multiple surgeons and saw the effectiveness of the procedures those surgeons chose to use during and after surgery. In this sense, the nurses were interchangeable, as all would be trained and skilled to assist all the surgeons.

Within this culture, the variance in procedures required the nurse to assume a slightly different professional identity with each surgeon they worked with. These various identities made them valuable to the individual surgeons but limited their effectiveness in the hospital setting.

With ZIOZ, Kathy was able to create a community among her fellow nurses. She encouraged them to talk about their observations and play a central role in achieving the goal of zero adverse events.

Before ZIOZ, the nurses had to follow each surgeon's chosen procedures, regardless of what the nurse thought was best. After ZIOZ, they were empowered to give input to surgeons because the nurses could speak with a unified voice and support each other as they worked toward a common objective.

This sense of community among the nurses created a powerful incentive for the surgeons to adhere to the ZIOZ procedures.

5. Communities Inform Systems

Community refines and reinforces our identities. In that way, communities amplify the voices of many individuals by helping them express their desires and concerns in a unified way.

ZIOZ was a system, but it was simple and structured to encourage input from people outside the orthopedic clinic. As a result, Mark and Kathy began to look at other departments in the hospital to identify where they could contribute to ZIOZ.

Systems influenced by the shared concerns of a community make broader changes that contribute to scale.

To continue to scale, systems must work together. The orthopedic clinic was a system inside the larger hospital system. That hospital was, in turn, a system inside the larger U.S. healthcare system. The U.S. healthcare system was also part of the global healthcare system.

For ZIOZ to continue to scale, the community it created had to influence the larger hospital system. This happened when Kathy approached other departments that were part of these patients' care and sought to involve them in the ZIOZ program. She represented the community of nurses created by ZIOZ in the orthopedic clinic.

Influencing the hospital system allowed ZIOZ to scale. That scale created opportunities for Mark and Kathy to speak at conferences and influence the U.S. and global healthcare systems.

The rapid growth of ZIOZ in other hospitals worldwide was evidence that it was a system that created scale. Its inclusion in the development of integrated clinical pathways and the software systems that deployed them shows how ZIOZ became a fundamental part of surgical care in less than 10 years.

The Cycle Becomes a Movement

The last step of the cycle determines if scale becomes a movement. If a community is allowed to inform the further development of a system, that community often moves from being users to becoming evangelists.

Tech companies like Apple, Microsoft, and Google have perpetuated their growth and innovation by embracing the community of developers who are the most committed users of their products.

Unfortunately, this did not happen with ZIOZ. The nurses were the most invested community, but they did not have a voice in how the hospital attempted to develop and deploy ZIOZ to other types of surgery. Instead, ZIOZ was absorbed into software programs that helped manage patient care.

The system ZIOZ created scaled everywhere these larger systems scaled, but the impact on culture, identity, and community was lost. The best procedures were codified and became the default options for every patient whose care was managed by the software. This was a huge gain. But the experience of the doctors and nurses working together to provide better care was lost in the process.

"ZIOZ was the biggest morale boost to the orthopedic surgery nurses," Kathy told me. "Those who are still there are sad it is no longer being used in the same way." In place of the dynamic community of individuals working together to care for patients and save lives, nurses now have an interchangeable and impersonal electronic order set.

Mark was also deeply disappointed that ZIOZ did not start a movement in patient care at his hospital, even though it had become part of the integrated clinical pathways that would guide the care provided to millions of patients. But by this time, he was already thinking about how God might use ZIOZ to advance the gospel.

But before we return to that story, it will be helpful to consider how the cycle applies to the beginning of the movement of Christianity as recorded in the New Testament.

Scale in the Bible

Scale and Faith

Scale influences how we see the world and what we think is possible. In this way, scale has affected our faith.

Faith is "the assurance of things hoped for, the conviction of things not seen" (Hebrews 11:1). Scale has taken "things not seen" and made them part of our everyday lives, and it has taken "things hoped for" and placed them within our reach.

Healing is an obvious place where this happens. The Gospels are full of accounts of how Jesus healed others. Faith was closely linked to healing in both Jesus' and the early church's ministry (Luke 7:22, James 5:14-16).

Today, many diseases, including leprosy, have been eliminated or are easily diagnosed and treated. But medicine cannot provide patients and healthcare providers what an individual relationship with their loving Creator can.

As people created in God's image, we are constantly working to reduce the effects of the fall on creation. Scale is one way we do this by providing clean water, electricity, medical care, and other essentials for life to more and more people. Yet scale cannot remove the effects of sin in us.

As we use scaled goods and services, we allow the focus of our hearts to shift away from providing for our basic needs to meeting our spiritual needs. We can use that abundance to pursue our relationship with God and others. Otherwise, we end up feeling anxious, purposeless, and isolated.

We must resist the temptation to believe that our spiritual needs can be met in the bounty of scaled products and services. Seeing scale in the Bible can help us do that.

Scale in the Bible

Scale in the Bible starts at the very beginning. God created an environment where plants could thrive, and swarms of creatures could live and reproduce.

God created plants "yielding seed according to their own kinds, and trees bearing fruit in which is their seed, each according to its kind" (Genesis 1:12). God created all kinds of sea creatures and birds and told them, "Be fruitful and multiply and fill the waters in the seas, and let birds multiply on the earth" (Genesis 1:22).

We read four times that God created "according to its kind" (Genesis 1:12, 21, 24, 25). Every living thing God created had the ability to reproduce exponentially. Science has helped us discover many of the interchangeable chemical processes that make this life possible.

When God created man and woman, he also commanded them to reproduce. But, unlike the animals, God did not create a swarm of people. He created only two. The first man and woman were called to reproduce in the community we call the family and under God's particular care (Genesis 2:22-25).

The rest of Genesis follows these families, first the dependents of Adam and Eve, then Noah, and then Abraham, who became the nation of Israel. That nation grew and encountered the ancient world's great civilizations, including Egypt, Assyria, Babylon, Greece, and Rome.

But God had another purpose in mind for a spiritual family made up of people from "every tribe and language and people and nation" (Revelation 4:9). The movement of Christianity would accomplish this redemptive purpose.

The Scale of Acts 2

The beginning of the Christian movement is in Acts 2, starting on the Day of Pentecost. The story begins with the disciples gathered in an upper room in Jerusalem. "Suddenly a sound like the blowing of a violent wind came from heaven and filled the whole house where they were sitting. They saw what seemed to be tongues of fire that separated and came to rest on each of them. All of them were filled with the Holy Spirit and began to speak in other tongues as the Spirit enabled them." (Acts 2:2-4)

In response, the disciples ran out into the street and amazed the crowd already in Jerusalem for the Feast of Pentecost by speaking in languages these travelers could understand.

Then Peter addressed the crowd. He announced that Jesus' crucifixion was not a failure but was part of God's plan to conquer sin. Jesus was the one for whom the nation of Israel was waiting. But, instead of seeing this, the people had rejected him and participated in his death.

This message and the miraculous signs had a dramatic effect. The Bible says that the listeners were "cut to the heart" and asked the disciples, "What should we do?" (Acts 2:37). Peter immediately told them to "repent and be baptized, and receive the Holy Spirit" (Acts 2:38).

The effect was explosive. In one day, the disciples went from a group of about 120 (Acts 1:15) to about 3,000 (Acts 2:41).

Scale made this movement possible, as we can see in the cycle of scale.

Systems Create Scale in the New Testament

Jesus lived and died when two primary systems ruled Israel. The first was the religious system based on the Old Testament law. The scribes, pharisees, priests, and elders controlled this system. Judaism at this time had become a complex set of rules that dictated almost every area of life.

This system was specifically built *not* to scale. You had to be born a Jew and maintain a ritually pure lifestyle, which was costly. In addition, Jews were not trying to get other people to convert to Judaism.

Instead, they held clear boundaries between themselves and outsiders. Relationships between the Jews and other groups were often hostile.

Jesus consistently ran afoul of these rules. He saw the hypocrisy of the religious leaders who had created an impersonal system instead of one that drew people into a relationship with God. Jesus preached a gospel of forgiveness and freedom from slavery to the law and of a God who knew each of his children individually.

But Israel also lived under another system, the occupying army of the Roman Empire. Rome was the largest empire to that point in history, having scaled its control to more of the known world than any previous conqueror.

One reason Rome scaled was their interchangeable approach to religion. Rome worshiped the emperor but allowed existing religions to continue in the lands it conquered, so long as the religion didn't supplant emperor worship.

Rome also developed a network of roads that allowed it to move troops and information around its empire. This interchangeability allowed Rome to scale its control over many different nationalities.

Rome was an impersonal and oppressive system for the Israelites.

Scale Shapes Culture in Israel

Rome's ambition to scale conflicted with Israel's determination to remain exclusive. Jesus stepped right into this conflict.

Combining these two systems created a particular culture in first-century Israel. The Jewish people understood themselves to be God's chosen people living under the oppressive rule of a pagan army. As a result, they were keenly interested in anyone who sounded like a Messiah.

Rome's presence heightened the Jewish people's expectations of the Messiah's coming, as did stories of Old Testament prophets who performed miracles and judges who raised and led armies. The Jews expected their Messiah to be a military leader and prophet, whereas Jesus came for a different purpose.

Jesus drew large crowds with his teaching. He spoke in parables related to people's day-to-day experiences and performed miracles. Jesus' teaching and ministry resonated with those caught between the demands of the religious leaders and Roman control.

But Jesus did not use his influence to make himself comfortable like the religious leaders. Nor did he turn his popularity into an uprising to change things by physical force.

Instead, Jesus spoke of being changed on the inside. He described the individual choices people must make to follow him. Through his teaching, he described what it meant to have a new identity. And, through his miracles, he proved he had the power to change people's lives.

But Jesus was not just another popular teacher. He came with another mission that only he could fulfill.

Culture Forms Identity in Judaism

Jesus had a unique identity that no one else could share. He was born into the culture of Judaism, but that was just the backdrop to his true identity.

Jesus was the only person in history to be fully God and fully man. How that worked is still a mystery to us, and the degree to which Jesus drew on his divine or human abilities is still debated.

But the Bible is clear that he was the Eternal Son of God, conceived by the Holy Spirit and born to a virgin. He lived a sinless life even though he faced temptation and suffered beyond what we can imagine.

Jesus was unique, yet he was still one of us. As the Son of God, Jesus was in relationship with his Heavenly Father and the Holy Spirit. But he was also able to relate to his followers and friends.

Jesus is above any culture, but God used Judaism, a culture built around the system of the law, to clarify Jesus' unique identity. Jesus was the Great High Priest who made atonement for sin once and for all through his sacrifice of himself.

Only Jesus could fulfill the unique purpose of satisfying a holy God's need for justice while offering forgiveness and grace to those who would believe in him. God demonstrated that he accepted Jesus' sacrifice when he raised him from the dead.

When, by faith, we believe in who Jesus is and what he has done for us, we are changed. The New Testament tells us that when we trust in Christ, we are given a new identity as God's children.

Identity Becomes Community

After his resurrection, Jesus did not remain on earth. He explained to his followers that there was another way he would always be with them.

Even with his resurrected body, Jesus could only be in one place at one time. But he promised that after he left, he would send his Spirit, who would be with us always and everywhere.

That's what happened in Acts 2. Jesus' presence returned through the Holy Spirit and filled the small group of followers huddled in the upper room. With new boldness and power, they burst into the street and began to share the good news with everyone who would listen.

At that moment, the identity of being a follower of Jesus changed. Before the Holy Spirit, his followers were the 120 people in the upper room who had been with him during his life. But after Pentecost, the identity of a Christ-follower became someone who believed, got baptized, and was filled with the Holy Spirit. The size of that community would only be limited by God's purpose.

The identity change experienced by Jesus' followers was supernatural, and the result was a new type of spiritual community.

Community Informs Systems

Because the gospel speaks to the need for a relationship with our creator, it can translate into every culture and language. As the gospel spread in the first century, more and more non-Jews were being saved.

The Apostle Paul used his knowledge of Jewish and Roman law to explain the Gospel to those in Greek culture. His message at Mars Hill (Acts 17:16-34) started with describing the cultural and religious categories the Romans knew instead of using categories from Judaism.

Paul also used his Roman citizenship after he was arrested in Jerusalem to appeal for a hearing before Caesar. As a result, many Romans with positions of influence at the highest level of the Empire heard the gospel and became believers (Phil. 4:22).

In this way, the community of the church influenced the development of the Roman Empire. That influence reached a historic level in 800 AD when Charlemagne became the first Christian Emperor of Rome, and Christianity became the official religion of the Holy Roman Empire.

From there, the Christian community heavily influenced the Western system of government through the Middle Ages. That system preserved the teaching of the apostles and early church fathers. Centuries later, Martin Luther and other key people of the Protestant Reformation rediscovered them. The printing press allowed these beliefs to be shared widely, helping them scale.

God formed his church out of the scale made possible by the Roman Empire. The church went on to have a greater impact on human history than any other group or system of belief.

So where is that happening today?

12

Scale in Sustainable Med

Mark was looking for a connection between his faith and how he had seen ZIOZ scale. He believed it was there, and he had seen people of faith, like Kathy, embrace what he was doing. But he wanted his work to bring others to faith and to help them live their faith in new ways.

Mark knew a spiritual dynamic was missing in the orthopedic surgery clinic. Faith defined his life, first as a follower of Jesus and then in how he practiced medicine. However, these shared priorities were uncommon among the other doctors who had worked with him.

ZIOZ had failed to change the hearts and minds of many doctors who used it. This troubled Mark deeply. He was committed to providing the best care, but there were challenges in the culture and identities that ZIOZ could not overcome. Some people wouldn't change their minds no matter how clear the evidence was.

Mark wanted to change people, not just procedures. Moreover, his identity as a Christ-follower meant that he wanted to have an impact on others for eternity, not just for their health in this life.

A longing was growing in Mark's heart to see the ZIOZ system deployed through an army of Christ-following medical workers and through the spiritual community of the church.

NTDs as a Failure of Scale

Before we examine Sustainable Med's story through the cycle of scale, let's consider how NTDs demonstrate the harmful effects of this scale.

1. Systems Create Scale

The medical systems in Africa and other underdeveloped parts of the world fail to scale medical services. Despite having access to Western funds, technology, and training, they cannot sustain a treatment approach that addresses the most prevalent diseases affecting their people. An interchangeable and impersonal Western medical system does not work in these undeveloped nations.

2. Scale Shapes Culture

This failed medical system prevents care from scaling effectively in underdeveloped countries. In addition, the chronic lack of resources to support this Western-influenced system forces doctors and leaders to prioritize short-term survival over any meaningful effort that could make a long-term difference. As a result, there are no cultural categories for doctors or healthcare workers to understand themselves as working for the best care of the individuals they treat.

3. Culture Forms Identity

This lack of healthy cultural categories means that everyone working in the system has developed an identity formed by ignorance and misunderstanding. This includes the medical workers and those suffering from NTDs. Both were ignorant about the widespread, well-known infections. As a result, medical workers didn't understand the need for treatment, and those infected didn't know what their quality of life should be.

4. Identity Becomes Community

Because of these unhealthy identities, the impoverished communities adopted NTDs into their view of the world. And the lack of care from the medical community reinforced the idea that NTDs were an unavoidable part of life. As a result, medical professionals viewed any ongoing effort to address NTDs with skepticism. And the solutions they did bring were never embraced by the people who had the diseases.

5. Communities Inform Systems

Since all previous treatment efforts had been short-lived, communities had learned to get what they could from new treatment programs but did not expect them to make any meaningful difference. Illness persisted, and as a result, these communities could not rise out of poverty and had no basis for informing the system that was failing them.

This failure at scale reinforced the conclusion that NTDs were not curable and not worth the effort. This lack of hope distorted these impoverished communities' entire economic and social structure.

This was the problem that Sustainable Med faced.

Sustainable Med's Success at Scale

With this failure of scale as a backdrop, let's look at the cycle of scale and how Sustainable Med successfully applied it.

1. The ZIOZ System Created Scale

Mark knew ZIOZ worked, and he was confident it could work for NTDs. ZIOZ was a simple process that allowed other systems to work together better. It created an environment where everyone involved in a patient's care could exchange ideas. And it empowered those caring for the patients to have a say in which procedures should be used.

ZIOZ was simple enough to teach to African healthcare workers, yet it had proven its effectiveness in eliminating adverse outcomes facing the most advanced medical systems in the world.

2. Scale Shapes a Culture of Eradication

Systems create scale. But in many situations, its impact on culture is an afterthought.

Mark and his Sustainable Med team rejected that approach early on. They knew they could not scale a process simply by committing more resources to the problem. They didn't have those resources, and they saw that the Western NGOs' impersonal approach to NTDs was ineffective. In fact, they saw how it often made the problem worse.

Through the process of listening to the individuals afflicted with and fighting NTDs, the team made an important realization. In order to eradicate the diseases, they had to focus on eliminating the need for treatment.

Scaling a treatment would always be a losing battle because a lack of knowledge about NTDs and how they spread would continue to cause infections. However, ZIOZ was a process to eradicate infections by removing their causes.

Simply tweaking the approach tried by other organizations would not be enough. Sustainable Med must form a new culture of disease eradication. Medical workers and pastors needed new categories to understand the problems caused by NTDs and themselves as individuals.

Mark knew that not every trainee would adopt these new categories and help scale ZIOZ as he envisioned. But he was confident ZIOZ would inspire some individuals to see its potential.

3. Culture Forms a Caring Identity

The trainees needed to take a new culture back with them, but how would that change the people in their communities who didn't attend the conference?

The existing culture of accepting NTDs made people more likely to keep repeating the same choices, even with new information. Making new choices would mean going against years of tradition and socially accepted behaviors.

New information is rarely enough to make us choose something different. We need to experience the difference those choices will make in our lives in order to risk something new. That experience happens through interacting with someone who cares for us in a different way.

Mark and the team realized that Neglected Tropical Diseases were, first and foremost, diseases caused by neglect. To treat this neglect, the trainees had to be relational with those affected by NTDs. The goal was to bring them the good news of a relationship with their creator. NTDs prevented that message from getting through.

The trainees had to care for others like the Sustainable Med team cared for them. That meant they had to act and relate to others differently when they returned from their training. During the training they had been treated as those who could own the problem and develop the solutions. This was the effect of being treated as those created in God's image, which was a new experience for many.

By focusing on spiritual identity change, Sustainable Med was creating a spiritual movement rather than just scaling medical processes.

4. Identity Becomes a Community Leaders

The trainees learned about NTDs and how to eradicate them by using the ZIOZ problem-solving and innovation process, which aims to build community ownership of the problem and the solution.

Sustainable Med leaders modeled a culture of eradication, which helped form the identities of some of the trainees. Now, the team had to let trainees go and see what they did with that.

As the team tracked what happened, they noticed that trainees who returned to their communities and immediately put their training into practice made the biggest difference.

As a result, ZIOZ began inviting people to their training conferences who had a desire to be involved in their community. These individuals demonstrated a willingness to use their existing relational networks to treat NTDs.

However, the trainees didn't always apply what they'd learned the first time. Sometimes, they needed many follow-up conversations and additional instruction. "This approach requires deep investments into relationships," Mark would say.

Sustainable Med began to shift ownership to those leaders who had demonstrated their commitment to the organization's central values. Mark and others began referring to these men and women as partners— people who shared God's love by removing the barriers NTDs created to the gospel.

The conferences and follow-up built a strong community among these partners, which supported their new identities.

5. Communities Inform Health Systems

The training's effect was encouraging, as the number of people trained and impacted each year grew steadily. Sharing stories of what worked and didn't work helped everyone see the various ways ZIOZ could be applied, inspiring them to use it wherever they could.

Between 2016 (when Sustainable Med named its first Leaders of Excellence) and 2018, Sustainable Med nearly doubled the number of trainees to almost 3,000. But it only added four staff members in Africa.

The program's sustainability is evident in that second- and third-generation trainees now lead most of the training. This was the exponential effect that would create a movement.

By 2022, Sustainable Med had 15 Leaders of Excellence across seven African countries. These individuals collectively trained over 15,000 individuals, bringing the total number of trained individuals to almost 40,000.

By the end of 2023, those 40,000 trainees had impacted nearly 4 million people with meaningful help toward NTD eradication. Leaders of Excellence had increased the number of people trained by an average of 150% per year between 2015 and 2023!

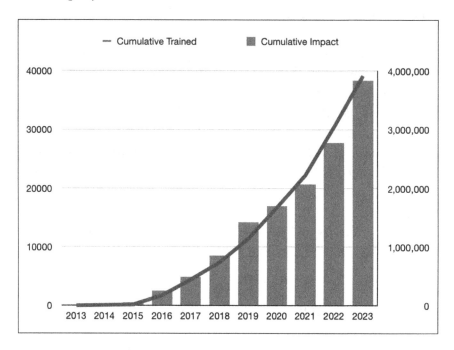

Medical systems in these regions took notice. As we've already seen, God was giving Sustainable Med opportunities to influence how NGOs and national health departments view and combat NTDs.

In response, these systems changed how they would treat NTDs and scale their solutions. More impoverished communities in Africa became economically healthier and more people could live healthy, productive lives.

The Impact of Scale

Sustainable Med was achieving scale.

ZIOZ proved to be an interchangeable system that could adapt to the many situations that caused NTDs. It no longer required the Team's direct involvement, as second- and third-generation trainees were individually grasping what ZIOZ could accomplish.

The culture of disease eradication was overcoming the culture of NTD acceptance. ZIOZ helped people ask what happens before, during and after an adverse event. And the cycle of innovation helped them understand themselves as people who could come up with their own solutions.

This culture of eradication formed identities that became communities that worked together to own the problem and identify the solutions. As a result, solutions were sustainable and had a dramatic effect.

The most dramatic effect has been in Rwanda, the African nation where Sustainable Med has grown quickest.

- Government partnered with Christian leaders to help people change self-destructive behaviors.
- People cared for others and overcame a culture of indifference and suspicion.
- Christians helped eliminate institutional waste and corruption.
- The communities helped by Sustainable Med welcomed others and shared their knowledge and resources.
- Leaders from other faiths have asked Christians to teach their people because of the love they brought.
- The gospel has reached millions of people who lived within sight of a church but had never experienced the love of Jesus.

Sustainable Med was able to scale a process that started a movement of Christ-followers who worked through the church to remove the barrier to the gospel caused by NTDs.

But can this same approach to scale be used in other places to solve other problems?

Curing Donkey Bites

"ZIOZ helped cure donkey bites," Emmanuel told me. "It doesn't just work on NTDs." He said this with pride, even though curing donkey bites was never part of Sustainable Med's vision.

"We had a partner who went to a village in his region," he recalled. "As he began asking questions about the villagers' health, he saw donkey bites as the biggest problem."

The partner also saw evidence of NTDs, so he faced a choice. Should he disregard the donkey bites and focus on what he knew? After all, none of the training or resources he had from Sustainable Med had talked about donkey bites.

Although he may not have been trained to eradicate donkey bites, he had been empowered to help people take ownership of their problems and develop solutions. So, he began to ask what happened before, during, and after the donkey bites.

As he listened to the responses, the picture soon became clear. The village water supply was several miles away. The villagers used donkeys to carry the water cans. By the time they approached the village with full cans, the donkeys were tired and dehydrated, and the villagers were impatient to get home.

"The donkeys would want to stop, and the people would need to push them to go," Emmanuel recalls. "So, the donkeys bit them." These bites would get infected and cause significant health problems.

Once ZIOZ had revealed the cause of the problem, the village could identify the solution, which was to have a water supply in the village. Sustainable Med could help with that, and while the work was being completed, they provided carts to make it easier for the donkeys to move the water and make fewer trips.

"The villagers had NTDs as well," Emmanuel states. "But while they were dealing with infected donkey bites, those were not their concern."

Improving the lives of donkeys was not part of the mission. But this village depended on donkeys to survive, so caring for the villagers meant caring for their animals.

So, how do we use this approach to scale to solve other problems we see in the world?

PART 3
How God Uses Scale

Redemptive Scale

How Does God Change the World?

Mark wrestled with a question familiar to many of us: What role do we play in God's work of changing the world? Or, put another way, how does God change the world through us?

If you are a person of faith, you should ask this question regularly. But we must trust how God chooses to use us and our abilities.

God is all-powerful and has a plan that includes all things. He "works in us to will and do according to his good pleasure" (Philippians 2:13). That means no act of love and kindness toward another is too small to honor him.

But sometimes, God makes us aware of a bigger problem that doesn't allow us to be content with what we are doing now. Sometimes, God gives us a glimpse into something he's doing, and with that glimpse comes the conviction that we can play a part.

That happened to Mark in 2010 when he learned about the one billion people who suffered from NTDs. The story of Sustainable Med is how God used Mark to scale ZIOZ to begin to help remove a barrier to the gospel for one billion people.

He couldn't have accomplished this by simply scaling ZIOZ or Sustainable Med. Rather, he needed to start a movement to help love and care for people suffering from NTDs.

Scaling Love and Care for People

Scale and love are fundamentally different. No system can love a person; only another person can. Systems scale to solve a need. Love is caring for another above yourself.

Care can be scaled in a practical sense. We see all kinds of technology that promises to care for people, from robots for the elderly to chatbots that answer our customer service questions. ZIOZ scaled and became part of a standard system of care in orthopedic surgery.

Systems can be scaled to respond to our needs. But responding to a specific need doesn't require love. Someone will do it if there's enough of an incentive.

That said, a loving person can extend their care for others by scaling a system that meets a specific need. Mark did that with ZIOZ in the hospital. Other people, driven by a desire to help others with a problem they personally experienced, might do the same by starting a support group or service.

But scaling a way to care for other's needs is not the same as scaling love for others. Scaling care can scale opportunities to show love. But to show love, the people providing care must move beyond caring for a need to caring for the person with the need.

For those of us who know Christ, love and care for others must be defined by God's purpose of redemption. Redemption is only accomplished through the gospel, which tells us we are separated from God by our sin and that faith in Christ is the only way to restore that relationship with him as our loving heavenly Father.

The growth of God's family is a movement guided by the Holy Spirit. But scale can contribute to supporting this movement.

Scale That Creates Movements

The ability to cure donkey bites illustrates how Sustainable Med empowers its partners to solve problems, even those unrelated to NTDs. The donkey bites had to be solved before the NTDs could be treated.

ZIOZ worked to remove the barrier to treating NTDs, which were still a barrier to sharing the gospel.

Scale that creates movements must be open-ended. The goal of scale in business often ends with forming identity, meaning your customers can't imagine their lives without your product or service. Your goal is to keep them in that limited view of their world. That may be good for your company's success but often works against the formation of communities that can inform the systems that create scale.

But if your desire is to better others' lives, the goal of scale must be empowerment. Empowerment makes a person's identity the turning point in scale. An empowered identity cannot be prescribed or limited. Empowered identities will become communities that will use whatever systems best serve their needs to accomplish their vision of good. Instead of the system controlling them, they ultimately control the system.

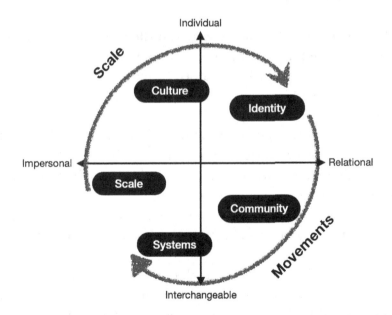

In this sense, scale controls the first half of the cycle. The culture shaped by scale will determine if the identities it forms are limited or empowered. If they are limited, communities may still form, but they will not influence the system, and the cycle will end. If they are empowered, they will form communities with other free individuals around a shared cause and find or adapt a system that serves that cause.

A business or organization can continue to serve that movement. If its scale helped create the movement, it is in a prime position to provide the resources it needs to grow. But this requires listening to the communities and adjusting its systems in response. The movement can drive further scale.

The greatest source of freedom and empowerment is a new identity in Christ. Since Sustainable Med wanted to be part of this movement, they had to empower their partners to live out that freedom in whatever way God led them.

Redemptive Scale creates movements that accomplish God's purposes in the world.

How God Uses Scale

We cannot fully account for what God allows to scale. Sometimes, God allows something to scale that reveals our depravity and tendency to reject him, such as the harm caused by modern weapons or social media. These experiences appear to overwhelm the good that is created by scale.

By contrast, God often does not scale something we think would genuinely help others. Instead, he reminds us of the simple things he has commanded us to do and asks us to trust him with the results. This can lead to frustration and disillusionment.

But sometimes, God does scale something that supports a movement to love and care for others. That is what he is doing through Sustainable Med.

Scale, as I've described it in the cycle of scale, can accomplish good or harm. What matters is how people participating in it choose to respond.

Understanding the cycle of scale is a powerful reminder that culture, identity, and community are at the core of scale. But that knowledge alone is not enough. Some key guidelines at each stage can help redirect the cycle toward redemptive movements, or what I call Redemptive Scale.

I've developed a simple device using the acronym SCALE to help us remember the guidelines.

S - Simplify
C - Choose
A - Ask
L - Listen
E - Empower

We'll examine these principles in more detail and see how the Sustainable Med story illustrates Redemptive Scale.

14

<u>S</u>CALE - *Simplify*

Scale is not simple. It often requires creating multiple interdependent processes, and that is often a complicated endeavor.

But the overarching principles that coordinate and govern those processes must be simple. Otherwise, scale remains oppressive and burdensome to those who could benefit from it.

Joint replacement surgery is an example of this. Replacing a hip or knee is a complicated medical procedure. As a result, a certain percentage of adverse events, including death, were considered an acceptable risk.

However, Mark rejected that conventional wisdom and prayed for a way to care for his patients more effectively. In response, God gave him ZIOZ, which asked what happens before, during, and after a procedure contributing to these adverse events.

Mark described ZIOZ as a "novel, simple process improvement strategy." It didn't include any new medical procedures. But it aligned the procedures already in place to greater effect, which is why it scaled so quickly and effectively.

ZIOZ allowed for rapid innovation from multiple people around a unified goal. For that to happen, it had to be simple enough for everyone to understand.

The Missing Piece

ZIOZ has proven itself to be a simple tool for innovation, and Mark knew it could be used to eradicate neglected tropical diseases. It was simple enough that pastors and community healthcare workers could be trained to use it.

However, ZIOZ's simplicity did not guarantee its scalability. For ZIOZ to truly make a difference, it needed to empower these individuals to solve problems. Unfortunately, empowerment was not a shared value for those trainees.

This became evident during an early conference in Uganda. The Sustainable Med team worked through all the training modules they had developed on NTDs and ZIOZ, as well as the training on the Christian faith.

Then, they took time to ask the participants what they were missing so they could go and deploy what they had learned. At that point, someone raised his hand and said, "You expect us to come up with solutions. Africa is not known for its innovation."

This individual had identified innovation as the missing link. Without innovation, ZIOZ would not scale.

Faith and Innovation

Selin Waltz attended that conference in Uganda. She was a senior engineer working at Procter & Gamble, and she had met Mark at Hope Church. Selin had helped Sustainable Med develop its training modules and traveled with Mark, David, and Kathy on some of the listening trips.

"Trainees were being released to solve problems," Selin recalls, "but they didn't know problem-solving." This realization hit Selin hard, as she worked for a global leader in product innovation.

*Selin (left) and Kathy, Mark, and David meet
with pastors and leaders in Uganda.*

Selin persuaded Mark and the team that a lack of innovation was part of the bigger problem. All of the help and resources poured into NTDs by Western NGOs had corrupted the medical system and made the infected populations more dependent on future aid. This made African healthcare workers dependent on the West's innovation.

This was in direct opposition to Sustainable Med's message and mission. The team believed that people freed by the gospel could make a difference in their community. The more the team looked at what hadn't worked, the more they knew genuine faith was part of the answer.

Selin and the team knew that with the power of faith, the trainees could innovate in ways they didn't believe possible.

Teaching Innovation

Selin developed a simple and memorable innovation process that could be summarized as Cry, Eye, and Why.

Cry stands for *Pray to God regularly for insight, understanding, wisdom, and humility.* In Selin and Mark's view, this was the most important step because innovation begins with noticing a problem and caring about how it affects others. This reflects the biblical promise found in James 1:5: "If any of you lacks wisdom, let him ask God, who gives generously to all without reproach, and it will be given him."

Eye stands for *Notice how the problem affects others and how they respond.* "Find out what is going on where God has placed you," Mark would say. "Something has to touch you personally to sustain innovation." This meant observing objectively to learn from others.

Why stands for *Ask lots of questions.* This was the best way to learn from other's experiences with the problem. What's going on here? Why is this happening? When did this start? "Start following where the questions lead you," Mark would say. "That will guide you into detailed, deep observation."

Cry, Eye, Why was a simple way that Sustainable Med could introduce the idea of innovation.

Simplify Guides Scale

Simplify is an important guideline for scale that contributes to a redemptive movement for two reasons.

First, the simpler something is, the more people can use it. ZIOZ was a very simple idea, and it helped everyone, from janitors to surgeons, to work together. That was a key to its scale.

That simplicity meant Mark and the team could take the same idea and deploy it in rural, impoverished villages. It allowed them to train pastors and healthcare workers who had minimal training by Western standards.

That's why everyone at Sustainable Med likes the story of Henry and his pumpkin seeds. Doctors and engineers alike are amazed at what this janitor from rural Africa could accomplish with ZIOZ. That is the power of a simple idea!

For an idea to scale, it must remove barriers, not create them. Simple ideas appear intuitive to others, who can easily adopt and use them as their own.

That's not good if you are trying to control what happens to your idea. But it is good if you want it to create scale. The simple approach helps people and can become part of a movement used by God.

Simplify Leads to Humility

Simplifying also helps us be humble. Mark quickly gave God the credit for ZIOZ and let students like Lincoln share the spotlight.

I'm not saying complicated things can't scale or that someone with a simple solution can't be arrogant. But when a system is simple enough for others to take ownership, it presses us to be humble and allow them to do so.

This is consistent with how God works. The gospel is simple enough to be understood by a child but profound enough to keep us marveling at its truth our entire lives.

In Acts 4, we read how Jesus's disciples astonished the "rulers and elders and scribes" because "they were uneducated, common men." As a result, these elites "recognized that they (the disciples) had been with Jesus" (Acts 4:5-13).

Later, the Apostle Paul would write, "But God chose what is foolish in the world to shame the wise; God chose what is weak in the world to shame the strong; God chose what is low and despised in the world, even things that are not, to bring to nothing things that are, so that no human being might boast in the presence of God." (1 Corinthians 1:27-29)

The things God chooses to use often appear foolish and weak in their simplicity. But those are often the very things that scale and create movements that love and care for others. Simplicity guides Redemptive Scale.

SCALE - Choose

The need to simplify requires choosing what is essential to your goal. But choosing plays a much more fundamental role in scale—not just for those who build a system for scale, but for those who use it.

Scale presents a large number of people with the same choice. These people do not have to make exactly the same choice. Rather, an idea can scale by systematizing how a choice is made.

Amazon has scaled to be the dominant online retailer by reducing many complicated processes to a "Buy It Now" button. The company's system is constantly managing the logistics and operations that reduce shopping to a simple search and click.

The choices we have as a result of scale are a key indicator of whether that scale is redemptive or destructive. What are those choices, and how do we prioritize them?

Sustainable Med offered its trainees the choice: join a movement to remove the barriers to the gospel caused by NTDs. Choosing to join the movement would give trainees the opportunity to offer people the most important choice: to receive God's love for them through Christ.

Scale Shapes Culture

Choosing is essential for scaling love and care because choices determine whether scale enhances or diminishes people's humanity.

Choices form culture. When we choose one thing over another, we demonstrate what we value. When many people choose that thing, that thing becomes an established cultural value. Scale shapes culture because scale allows a group of people to make the same choice. That choice does not have to be the best choice we would make because we can choose the best alternative from among the options that are readily available to us.

This influence is evident in our daily lives, from our food choices to consumer goods to entertainment. Scale that gives us harmful choices diminishes humanity by shaping a harmful culture, but scale that gives us good choices enhances humanity by shaping a healthy culture.

This effect is seen most vividly in social media's digital scale. In that case, algorithms constantly update the choices presented to you based on the choices you made moments ago and with input from the choices of thousands or millions of other users.

These companies aim to keep your attention as long as possible, so they continue to feed you content similar to the last content you chose. They do not present you with opposing points of view or other interpretations of the same events.

As a result, the examples of scale that cause the most extreme harm take away the importance of choice and replace it with mindless repetition.

Changing a Culture

We are well acquainted with cultural problems created by scale's effect in the digital world of social media. But scale is arguably more harmful in the way NTDs have shaped the culture of the populations they afflicted.

Because the people afflicted with NTDs didn't know what was causing their suffering, their only choice was to rely on what they could see in their existing culture. That culture gave them categories as different as believing in witchcraft to their depending on Westerners.

These people had to learn to take responsibility for their own care. For that to happen, they needed new choices. Trainees with Sustainable Med offered that. But first, trainees had to experience new choices themselves. The conferences gave them time to think about how to apply ZIOZ to their community's problems.

Applying ZIOZ at the conference was a transformative experience. This transformation meant they would return to their communities with a newfound understanding of other explanations for NTDs. These other explanations meant there were new choices for how to respond to something they'd lived with their entire lives.

Empowered by Choice

Emmanuel was deeply invested in his community in Rwanda. He had seen the effect that the existing culture of disease acceptance was having on him and others.

Previous efforts to treat NTDs reinforced this culture of acceptance. A particular example was a 2015 national campaign in Rwanda to address an NTD caused by intestinal worms.

"Before the campaign, 99% of the people in my community had these worms," Emmanuel recalls. "Despite all the effort and money, the campaign only managed to reduce that to 97%, a mere 2% drop!" The campaign failed to reinforce the new choices the community could make, leading people to revert to their old habits.

But now Emmanuel saw the causes of NTDs, not just the effects. When he realized that a lack of clean drinking water was his community's biggest problem, he was empowered to ask for access to the pipe running through his village.

Emmanuel's choice to address the root cause of the NTD had a ripple effect. By eliminating a major cause of the disease, its eradication became a real possibility. The visible impact of Emmanuel's choice sparked a culture of eradication in his community, inspiring others to take action.

But Emmanuel needed to encourage this culture of eradication further by engaging his community to participate even more.

Shaping a Culture of Eradication

The clean water supply had addressed one of the biggest needs, but that alone wouldn't change the culture. Emmanuel knew that 97% of his people were still dealing with this parasite. With a freshwater supply, he could apply ZIOZ to treat the problem in a sustainable way.

As Emmanuel began to guide the community through the ZIOZ process, they identified hand washing as the key preventative step. The intestinal worms carry soil-based parasites. People picked up fruit and potatoes from the ground and ate them without washing their food or their hands.

Handwashing was part of the government program, but it was futile without clean water. However, with the introduction of the new water supply, the situation changed dramatically. A central storage tank on the church property meant clean water was now readily available, which made hand-washing a viable and effective preventive measure.

"Now, when we tell people to wash their hands in clean water, the water is there," Emmanuel exclaims. "And when you tell them to drink clean water, it is there!"

The system of valves and pipes gave the community a choice of clean water. As more people made that choice, their choices shaped a new culture.

As a pastor, Emmanuel worked with the other village leaders to provide a way for each home to have a simple hand-washing station to use the clean water they brought from the church. Residents paid a small sustainability fee for accessing the water supply, so every home in the community had ownership of the clean water solution.

The impact of this ZIOZ process has been profound. When the community was retested for intestinal worms the following year, the infection rate had plummeted to 35%!

This significant drop is a testament to the effectiveness of the culture of eradication, which was shaped by the choice to own the problem and solution. People were no longer satisfied with a culture of disease acceptance. They were creating a culture of eradication by making new choices.

Choosing Guides Scale

For someone to take ownership of an idea or a problem so they can own the solution, they must see it as their choice. That resonates with our human dignity as those created in the image of God.

Behind the scenes, Sustainable Med funding helped the church provide something to the community that changed people's lives. Now, people were coming to the church daily for clean water, so it was natural for them to stay and hear about God's love for them.

"Jesus gets the credit first, and the community gets it second," Emmanuel says. "Sustainable Med stays invisible. They say, 'You tell us what the problem is, and we'll help you come up with a solution.' They don't tell you how to fix it."

By giving those afflicted with NTDs the choice to own the problem, Sustainable Med helped them scale the solution. Choosing guides Redemptive Scale.

SCALE - Ask

Simplify allows others to use your ideas to own the problem and the solution. Yet, it's easy to overlook asking about their needs or how the problem impacts them.

We might have an idea of how we would solve their problem from the outside, whether that is a neglected tropical disease or a simple personal problem we observe. But trying to scale a solution for them that makes sense to us is often a recipe for failure. We are not experiencing the problem, so our solution will address what we perceive its effect to be, which is often very different from what it is. This risks failure and should make us pause and reconsider our approach.

Often, we are in too much of a hurry to ask or too enamored with our own ideas to allow someone with a different experience to critique them.

These reasons for not asking are a lack of humility and compassion. We see people as problems to be solved, not those made in God's image.

The Failure to Ask

Many NGOs' past efforts to treat NTDs failed to ask for input from those living with the diseases. Their teams drew conclusions based on their observations and developed solutions that made sense to them but didn't work.

As a result, their efforts often made the situation more frustrating and discouraging for those living with the NTDs. This ineffectiveness also reinforced dependence on money from the West, which led to corruption.

"African countries have a lot of corruption," Emmanuel explains. "The local chief will pressure the NGOs to pay him for access." This drains money from the work and contributes to the high cost of Western organizations operating in the region.

For this reason, many NGOs avoid dealing with local chiefs and other leaders. In contrast, Sustainable Med chooses to make them part of the process from the beginning by asking them what problems they see in the community.

"We get the local chief, police, military, and health center leaders of the community involved and get to know them and tell them what we are trying to achieve," Emmanuel continues. "Even if they are suspicious, once we prove it is for the community, they help and support us."

That support begins with the simple act of asking.

Ask Good Questions

ZIOZ was built around three simple questions: What happened before the problem? What happens during the problem? What happened after the problem?

Selin's Cry, Eye, Why innovation process starts with asking God for wisdom, then noticing others, and ends with asking lots of questions. Asking good questions is foundational to everything Sustainable Med does. As a result, Sustainable Med leaders teach trainees this vital skill.

Early on, this wasn't always the case. When someone raised a concern in a discussion group during the training, the impulse of other participants was to respond with an answer. That seemed most helpful at the moment but did not help the person with the concern develop problem-solving skills.

The Sustainable Med team began including content that would help the leaders ask good questions. The effect was just what the team was hoping for.

"Giving an answer was short-circuiting the innovation process by jumping to a conclusion," David said. "We wanted peers to come alongside one another to empower and equip. The effect was amazing! We could see them developing each other right in front of us."

What Makes a Question Good?

It takes some effort to ask good questions. Like the trainees, we all want to jump in with a solution instead of helping that person become a better problem solver.

Good questions don't assume you know the answer. They focus on the other person by starting with, "When did you…" or "How have you…"

Open and Closed Questions

Questions can be open or closed. A closed question contains the expected answer already and only allows for a yes or no response.

Don't you think this topic is important?

That's a closed question. I clearly think it's important, and all you can do is agree or disagree. Closed questions stop the flow of conversation or start an argument.

An open question makes the other person the expert and cannot be answered yes or no. We need to think about what our question is accomplishing. How does it help the other person see the situation differently? It requires humility to really care about what the other person thinks.

When have *you* been asked a question that made you think?

That's an open question. You're the expert, as no one else can answer it for you. You can't answer it with yes or no. Open questions start conversations and lead to understanding.

Jesus asked many open questions, including when he asked his disciples, "Who do people say that I am?" (Mark 8:27). That question started a conversation, which ended with Peter confessing, "You are the Christ." (Mark 8:29)

A good rule of thumb is to start your questions with who, what, when, where, why, and how. These are open-ended questions that will help you respond with humility.

Ask About Suffering

Good questions are powerful and can be fun to ask. But when we see someone suffering, we tend to withdraw.

Suffering raises some of the hardest questions we face in our human experience. Nothing brings us to the limits of our abilities faster, and yet nothing connects us to every other human being more deeply.

Suffering creates an unresolvable tension in our lives. We should try to remove suffering wherever we can, but many types of suffering go beyond physical symptoms to emotional or spiritual pain that only God's love can heal.

As a doctor, Mark saw suffering every day. He did not assume that his patients' suffering required an explanation. He also cautioned his students and trainees to remember that patients needed more than an expert answer.

"They want someone to be there," Mark instructed. "We will act with compassion and comfort, which is minor to us but major to our patients!"

Mark tackled the question of suffering head-on. He talked about it with his medical students and demonstrated compassion for those suffering during his rounds. He made the question of suffering central in Sustainable Med's training.

Seeing people through God's eyes meant they had infinite value. This was the greatest lesson Mark would leave with those who knew him.

Ask For Change

Sustainable Med wanted to remove the barriers that NTDs created to the spread of the gospel. Good questions helped the organization alleviate the suffering these diseases caused.

These questions underscore the dignity and value of the person we are trying to help. And they demonstrate our humility by acknowledging we don't know all the answers, especially the answers only that person (the expert) can give.

There's a connection between identity and being asked a thoughtful question. Often, we don't know our identity because it's just who we are. Our identity is formed by the cultural categories we have been given to understand and explain ourselves and we have not spent much time thinking about it.

But when someone asks a question from a new perspective, it challenges those existing categories. Answering the question helps us create a new category to understand and explain ourselves.

A good question will draw us out and help us realize things about ourselves that we didn't see before. Asking a genuine, good question is one of the most affirming things we can do for another human being.

Being asked a good question helps us understand ourselves. It can strengthen and empower us and show us where we need help. Open questions can also help strengthen our sense of identity and motivate us to learn and develop further.

Asking Guides Scale

ZIOZ is three simple questions that create the choice of how to respond. Sustainable Med needed to find the right systems and people to scale that approach.

Scaling good questions seems counterintuitive. The key is not the quantity of the question but the quality. Often, a system that creates scale does so by eliminating questions.

Amazon eliminated the customer's logistical questions to focus on the most important decision: Buy it now. That is the only question that humans have to answer. The system can take care of everything else.

When someone wants to post a picture on Instagram, they can choose from just a few filters and effects, reducing the opportunity for creativity. But the essential question is relational: Who do you want to see this picture? By simplifying the artistic process and emphasizing sharing, Instagram achieved unprecedented scale.

For ideas to scale and create a movement, they must give others the genuine experience of owning a simple idea. Good questions invite them to do that, which is why asking guides Redemptive Scale.

SCA*LE* - Listen

It might go without saying that if we ask good questions, we need to listen to the answers. Yet listening is not automatic.

Asking a good question can affirm the dignity and humanity of the person we ask. But it's something else entirely to listen carefully to the answer.

Careful listening is a skill that can be taught, and we all benefit from practicing it. But there's a moment in some conversations when listening stops being a skill and becomes a connection. We are motivated to do that kind of listening because the person talking is someone whose perspective and experience matter to us.

We will naturally listen to a person with whom we share a common goal. If that goal is important to us, we intuitively sense that working with this person can make us more effective. But to get there, we must listen to each other.

When that type of listening happens, we have found someone who is pursuing the same objective. Our connection with that person might be the beginning of a community that cares about the same thing as us.

Community is part of scale because scale groups people together. But not everything that is called a community can contribute to a movement or is part of Redemptive Scale.

Defining Community

Community seems to be one of the most overused words in the English language at the moment.

"Community" has great marketing power. We all want to belong to something important and with people we admire. Advertisers have learned the art of presenting their product as essential to being part of that exclusive, desirable community.

We also use the word community to describe people and groups with whom we interact online. But as those "communities" have grown, so has our sense of loneliness and isolation. In one sense, we've expanded the definition of community so much that it's become meaningless. But the word itself is still important and worth clarifying.

"Community" is made up of the words "common" and "unity," meaning to be unified around what we have in common. Something in "common" can apply to many things, from a sports team to a particular software we use or where we live. What unifies us can be very basic, from wanting our team to win to getting our money's worth from a product or protecting the value of a house we own.

To make "community" more meaningful, we must be more specific about what we mean by "common" and "unity." That's where listening becomes essential—not just that we listen but whom we listen to.

Listening Defines Community

We are all created with the need to belong to something. In Genesis 1:26, "God said, 'Let us make man in our image.'" The plural "us" and "our" is the first indication that God is three-in-one, or the Trinity. The Trinity is community in its purest form, foundational to Christianity.

Because community originates in who God is, it has the power to heal. But because of sin, it can also hurt us. As a result, we are cautious about being drawn in because belonging to a community means being vulnerable to the harm that community can cause.

For that reason, we pursue community in stages. Initially, we listen to others in the community to learn what they value. But at some point, we must find a way to contribute ourselves. When we do, we hope others value our contribution.

We need to be heard, and we must listen to others. To engage with a community, you must make yourself known. In some way, you must speak, and they must listen.

This is true even of the most profound identity change of becoming a Christian. You may have trusted Christ as your Savior, but you must also engage with his community in the local church to grow in your faith.

When we realize we are part of a community that shares ownership of an idea, that idea becomes more important to us. As an idea becomes more important, we share it with more people.

In this way, community is both a driver and the outcome of scale.

The Power of Being Heard

When Lincoln presented at his first Sustainable Med conference, he was experiencing the community that would become critical to Sustainable Med's approach.

Instead of watching someone else present his work, he was invited to participate as a third-year medical student. Previously, he had voiced his thoughts about Sustainable Med's plans and contributed his ideas and questions. Now, he knew Mark and the team were listening to him because they were giving him the chance to speak.

Mark's conviction behind ZIOZ was that everyone in the orthopedic clinic had something to contribute to the patient's healthy recovery. He was now extending that approach to scaling ZIOZ to treat NTDs. That meant doctors, pastors, healthcare workers, and even students could participate in training one another.

Mark encouraged trainees to ask good questions and listen to their communities' experience of the problem to help them find the solution. He was modeling what it meant to learn from others, even though he was clearly the expert in the room.

Lincoln vividly remembers something Mark did that kept reinforcing that point. "We were discussing an NTD called schistosomiasis,"

Lincoln recalls. "Mark didn't know that the disease also went by the name bilharzia, but I did and told him that."

For the rest of the conference, whenever Mark talked about that NTD, he would stop and say, "Lincoln, what was the name of that disease again?" Lincoln would have to give the answer to the whole group.

"That always made me feel equal and valued," Lincoln remembers.

Transformed by Listening

The medical workers and pastors invited to the training had seen the negative effects of other NGOs' failure to ask and listen to those living with NTDs. They needed something different in Sustainable Med.

When the Sustainable Med team listened to them, they realized they were part of something bigger than themselves. By working through the ZIOZ process together, they began to feel the exponential effect of being part of a community that owned a revolutionary idea.

As the Sustainable Med team stayed in contact with the trainees, some took what they learned to another level by listening to and investing in others. They became Leaders of Excellence. These leaders attended the advanced conferences, which focused on community building. They shared stories of success, challenges, and information to help them be more successful, covering topics such as financial stewardship and leadership.

Most importantly, they broke into groups to discuss a problem they were facing in their local community. There, they analyzed the factors before, during, and after, and the group helped them refine their approach using ZIOZ.

What people said and heard during these advanced training conferences transformed many who attended. The experience of sharing and being heard empowered these leaders to do amazing things.

They were the ones who truly began to scale Sustainable Med and create a movement to love and care for others.

Listening Guides Scale

Sharing stories of what worked and what didn't became essential to the conferences. "Every community has something to share," Emmanuel said. "We can learn from the mistakes and successes of others."

This meant being willing to make mistakes and talk about them. But mistakes were part of the learning process. Those who were committed to loving and caring for their communities would find a way to overcome the obstacles.

Mark placed his confidence in the simple process of ZIOZ and the power of the gospel to change lives. That way, ZIOZ could scale in ways he would never have thought of himself.

ZIOZ was three simple questions, but the ability to listen made it a system that could scale redemptively. More important was the community it formed, which would be the beginning of a movement that would multiply Mark's impact in ways he could never accomplish on his own.

Listening guides Redemptive Scale.

SCALE - Empower

To love and care for someone else, a person must be loved and cared for themselves. The love they have received will move them to give that love to others.

Knowing that God, our Creator and Heavenly Father, loves and cares for us is the most powerful relational experience we can have. God's design is that we experience his love in the spiritual community of the church. As a result, spiritual communities are indispensable in scaling ideas that create movements that love and care for people.

Sustainable Med scales training by equipping pastors and Christian medical workers with the tools to eradicate NTDs. By inspiring people to engage their communities in figuring out the solutions to their problems, they empower these men and women to love and care for others in previously unimaginable ways.

To care for someone else above ourselves, we must be empowered to do so. That requires seeing ourselves as part of something bigger and having a greater purpose than meeting our own needs and making ourselves comfortable.

Empower is the last principle of Redemptive Scale.

Excitement and Joy

Starting a movement requires more follow-up than most training programs would provide. "Once people attend an initial training conference, our staff and key leaders continue to connect with and disciple them," David states.

This is demanding for the team. "It's hard," Emmanuel admits. "But what keeps me going is seeing people discover the excitement that there are solutions to their problems." That moment of empowerment is the spark of joy that sustains hope and moves the work beyond eradicating NTDs.

"To comprehend the question is half of the answer," he continues. "To hear them say "'I know what is going on, and what can be part of the solution.' That rules out witchcraft and superstition, which opens the door to trusting in God."

Those moments make it all worthwhile, and remembering how God worked in people's lives energizes the team to keep helping others.

"When I started out, I was scared," Lincoln admits. "All of a sudden, you see the big problem and limited resources, and it feels like a losing battle." Some trainees feel overwhelmed and quit, and relationships the team has invested in don't work out.

"The most helpful thing is to leave it all to Jesus Christ and put the stress on him," Lincoln says. "Then, the joy is amazing! You see people healed and incredible results from those you have invested in."

Emmanuel (left) and Lincoln (second from the right) with trainees

Staying Invisible

Considering Sustainable Med's impact in Africa, you could understand if Mark and the team wanted to ensure everyone understood the value of their work. But that's not the approach they chose to take.

Instead, Sustainable Med does everything it can to give its partners ownership and control, empowering its trainees. This even includes staying invisible to villagers while the work is being done.

"Jesus gets credit first, and the community gets credit second," Emmanuel states. "Once the trainees see Sustainable Med is not coming for the numbers and that they will be given a voice from the very beginning, that makes a huge difference."

Even those who receive a financial grant aren't required to promote Sustainable Med. Western funding often feeds local corruption, so the team has learned that staying invisible has clear advantages.

But that does not mean there is no accountability. Those who receive funds must provide detailed reports on their work and its impact.

Empowering Generosity

From the beginning, Mark wanted to emphasize the biblical concept of stewardship. Sustainable Med training materials include a business module on the topic, teaching that money and material goods are both a source of freedom and God's gift to us. Everything belongs to God, which means we are stewards, not owners.

The team wanted its partners and communities to feel ownership of their solution, not of the material goods and finances used to deploy it. When communities established a business to support the work of eradicating NTDs, Sustainable Med wanted them to prioritize consistency, quality, and trustworthiness, not profits.

The training taught trainees to be responsible with what they had by budgeting, building wealth with surplus income, and developing banking relationships.

This stewardship mindset was empowering. Even if a project

or business was unsuccessful, that failure would contribute to the community's knowledge. The burden of success was on God, not them.

Empowering Opportunity

Emmanuel had been raising pigs and cows he bought with a Sustainable Med grant but knew he wasn't getting all the value he could from his work. Shopkeepers at the local market often used dishonest scales. But there was even a bigger lost opportunity.

"When they slaughter a cow or pig, they sell all the meat at the same price," he says. "I realized there was a wasted opportunity to butcher these animals properly and sell the better cuts for a higher price."

Emmanuel knew that a proper butcher shop could be very successful. Emmanuel shared his idea with the team, and a Sustainable Med donor gave $55,000 for Emmanuel to start a meat processing plant with the highest standards of cleanliness, proper refrigeration, and honest scales. The plant, called Special Nyama, which means Special Meat, offers cuts and prepared meats not commonly available, such as filet mignon, New York strip, bacon, and sausage.

Patrick Singura, another Sustainable Med Leader of Excellence, manages the shop. The business plans to generate enough profit to support the work of about 70 long-term partners annually in Rwanda. In addition to contributing to Sustainable Med's long-term sustainability, Special Meat has created skilled jobs and increased the demand for livestock, which can now be sold at a higher price.

"We thank God for His amazing provision so far," Patrick says. "We have so many customers already because people know and trust Emmanuel and others who are involved."

Business has been so good that Patrick and Emmanuel are opening a larger facility and already have demand for all the meat they can process.

Empowerment Guides Scale

In Rwanda, the transformation of Etienne's village and the growth of Emmanuel's business are just the beginning. The movement continues to gain momentum because people are seeing and experiencing what life without NTDs can be and what freedom in the gospel can bring.

"Our work is restoring identities through training, equipping, and empowering local faith, medical, and community leaders," David summarized. "Not only are they given the tools for the work, but they are actively restored to their identities as true leaders."

Sustainable Med has scaled because it empowers the people it trains. To do this, you must trust the process. Mark trusted ZIOZ as an innovation process and the power of the gospel to change lives.

On their own, empowerment and trust would not have the same result. Combined, you get a type of empowerment that creates a redemptive movement. Empowerment guides Redemptive Scale.

Coming Full Circle

Sustainable Med illustrates how to scale a way to love and care for people. On the surface, the organization's story fits the framework I call the Cycle of Scale:

1. **Systems Create Scale:** ZIOZ was a proven method to overcome infections that made better use of the resources already in place.
2. **Scale Shapes Culture:** By asking what happened before, during, and after, ZIOZ established a culture of eradication toward neglected tropical diseases.
3. **Culture Forms Identity:** Understanding these diseases were preventable helped key leaders form an identity of ownership that they could take back to their impoverished communities affected by neglected tropical diseases (NTDs).
4. **Identity Becomes Community:** Empowered leaders spread a culture of eradication by engaging their communities in the innovation process.
5. **Communities Inform Systems:** Communities that owned the problem applied their solutions in sustainable ways that impacted their economic and social life.

However, the Cycle of Scale does not account for the impact Mark wanted Sustainable Med to have through the gospel. That impact came from the decision to focus on removing the neglect that made these diseases possible in the first place.

SCALE at Sustainable Med

When we look at Sustainable Med through the lens of Redemptive Scale, we can see how it created a movement that loves and cares for others.

S - Simplify

ZIOZ was a simple innovation process. For an idea to scale it must be simple. Then, many people can use it. Allowing others to take ownership of your process requires leaders to be humble, which honors God.

C - Choose

Sustainable Med offers trainees the choice to join a movement to remove the barriers to the gospel caused by NTDs. By developing solutions that would eradicate NTDs, the trainees could offer others the choice to live a healthier and more productive life.

A - Ask

ZIOZ was built around three simple questions: What happened before, during, and after the problem? Sustainable Med taught its trainees how to ask good questions, which was key to its effectiveness and growth as a movement.

L - Listen

Listening is hard work, and we naturally listen to other people who are pursuing what matters to us. A connection forms that can become a community, and our shared vision becomes more important to us. Being part of a community motivates us to share what we have with more people.

E - Empower

Building scale that creates a movement to love and care for people means empowering those living with the problem to solve it in their own and others' lives.

Redemptive Scale in Sustainable Med

Sustainable Med has scaled.

That scale alone has not fulfilled its vision, but the movement created by their Redemptive Scale has begun that work. The primary outcome for Sustainable Med would be sharing the gospel, but it did not train in evangelism as we think of it. Instead, by removing barriers to the gospel caused by NTDs, the natural result would be sharing the gospel.

This was not a shift from Mark's desire to use ZIOZ to treat NTDs. Instead, it was a realization that neglect, not diseases, caused neglected tropical diseases.

That neglect could only be overcome by caring for others more than yourself. In such a difficult environment, this was often an outgrowth of seeing your life's purpose to bring glory to God by building his kingdom. Only the gospel could produce that kind of life change.

God had already placed those with this spiritual vision within reach of these most impoverished communities. Their commitment kept them there to see the effect of their ZIOZ training take hold.

The church is God's chosen spiritual community that can help these impoverished people come to know him personally and live for his glory.

This critical difference set Sustainable Med apart: Scaling the eradication of NTDs served a greater mission. That mission was given by our Creator and is being carried out by a movement fueled by spiritual resources.

From the beginning, God has used scale to support and further this movement. God is using Redemptive Scale through Sustainable Med to continue that work.

Remembering Mark Snyder

Late in 2019, Mark noticed some weakness in his hands. He had surgery for a pinched nerve, but that didn't address the issue. Early in 2020, he was diagnosed with amyotrophic lateral sclerosis, or ALS (sometimes called Lou Gehrig's disease).

The disease moved quickly, and Mark passed away at the age of 69 on November 2, 2021. His funeral was held a week later at Hope Church.

Mark had prepared a video for his funeral. He told a bit of his story, including how he came to Christ in 1983 when he was 38 years old. "I needed God to change me," he said. Describing what had happened to him, he continued, "You go from someone who might want to do good to someone who has good living in them."

Kathy Levit, Mark's sister, shared what she remembered about the day he was diagnosed. "Mark said whatever God asked him to go through as a result of this diagnosis, he would do it to bring glory to God," Kathy said. "Mark was willing to let God use his life as a window for people to see the love and beauty of Christ, even if that meant suffering with ALS."

Emmanuel, Lincoln, and Stephen came to Cincinnati for the funeral. Stephen spoke about the many countries in Africa that Mark had impacted through Sustainable Med. "He was an amazing spiritual father who taught us how to read the Word of God," Stephen stated. "He mentored us in the world of science and innovation. He encouraged us to use our thinking ... both as medics and pastors.

"The greatest thing in this world is to know how to use what you have to make a difference," Stephen continued. "Mark is a man who came to this world with a purpose, and he has lived it."

Remembered for Love

Dr. Mark Snyder was a remarkable person who accomplished a great deal in his life and is remembered for what he accomplished. But, according to his own testimony, accomplishments are not the things Mark wanted to be remembered for. He wanted to be known for loving his wife, Carol, and their family.

Mark recognized how much God had given him, and he wanted to be a good steward. He also knew how much pain and suffering existed in the world, and that God has called us to be the hands and feet of Jesus.

What God values most are people created in his image. Each of us uniquely reflects our Creator, making us inherently valuable. Mark understood that.

How we approach scale ultimately reveals what we value. Mark had experienced the business approach to scale through his success with ZIOZ. But as a Christ follower, he placed the highest value on changed lives. That led him to pursue scale in a different way and to different ends.

Jonathan Burnham and Mark Snyder in 2020.

Mark wanted to further the movement of the gospel to share God's love with others. The story of Sustainable Medical Missions illustrates how God can use Redemptive Scale to do that.

"Who knows what my dad would have done if he were still alive," David wonders. "But that's not what God had planned for him."

The tragedy of Mark's death is tempered by the fact that we can see his life in full and begin to evaluate the impact of how he chose to live.

Scale and God's Love

Scale presents some of us who know Christ with a choice. Will we focus more on what we do in the world or on who we are?

If we focus on what we do, we might achieve some form of scale. But that scale may do more harm than good or be forgotten. But if we focus on who we are in Christ, we will experience his love for us, and that love will overflow in our lives and make us part of God's redemptive movement to share his love with others.

Redemptive Scale can create movements that love and care for people. It can empower those who want to solve the problems affecting other people's lives.

God may choose to use you to scale something good. If he does, I pray he uses the story of Mark Snyder and Sustainable Med to inspire and guide you as you show his love to others.

Printed in the United States
by Baker & Taylor Publisher Services